Laws Of The Universe Vol. 1

Don't believe nor disbelieve, simply have your own experience.

- Kevin S. Black

Laws Of The Universe Vol. 1

An Esoteric Understanding of Energy, Frequency and Vibration

By: **Kevin S. Black**

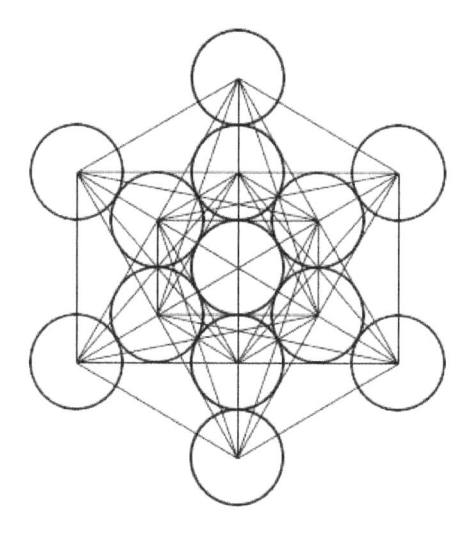

In his Laws of the Universe, Kevin Black has pulled together a thorough and insightful overview of the universal forces that impact all of humankind. Whether your interest is cosmic principles, sacred geometry, vibrations, numerology, mysticism, esoteric wisdom, or the law of karma, this volume provides the reader with a necessary handbook for what it means to be human—(spiritual beings having a physical experience.) It weaves together science, spirituality, and mysticism so that we might better understand the interplay between who we are and who we are meant to be. I recommend this personal roadmap for anyone interested in expanding personal consciousness."

-Kevin J. Todeschi, author of

- *Edgar Cayce on Mastering Your Spiritual Growth*

Preface

In ancient times our ancestors had knowledge that we are still trying to understand today and wisdom that stretched light-years ahead of their time. That alone is kind of amazing in itself. The mysterious origin of how they became introduced to this advanced knowledge is widely debated amongst scholars and scientists and remains to be a perplexing mystery that has continued to dwell in the unknown for thousands of years. Even though the ancients had knowledge that appears to be lost in time, there is absolutely one thing that still remains evidently clear to today, and that is our ancient ancestors had a very comprehensive understanding of energy, frequency and vibration. It truly seems clear that not only did our ancient ancestors have access to this advanced knowledge, but this knowledge was applied in some of the most sophisticated of ways. The ancients truly understood that together energy, frequency, and vibration are the basic foundations of everything that exist in the universe and beyond. This book was carefully and methodically put together to give you, the reader, a much deeper and more clear understanding of those natural forces that literally shape and bind everything in our physical and non-physical existence.

Author Kevin S. Black is both a student and researcher of spiritual esoteric teachings, as well as a talented audio/recording engineer with certifications from Berklee College of Music as well as Audio Institute of America. His field of study allows him to understand how frequency and vibration affects not just humans when we listen to music and different sounds, but also understand how vibration and frequency affects physical objects in their local environment and everything in our physical creation. What happens in the spiritual, manifest in the physical, it is the spiritual world or the immaterial world that both communicates and influences our three-dimensional reality.

In order for all of us to truly and fully understand what the ancient people comprehended about the physical world around them, we must do what they did and open our minds to more than just the physical world around us. You will slowly pull back the veil and see exactly what important role energy, frequency, and vibration play in the background of our reality throughout our busy day-to-day lives. You will also see how everything in physical creation comes from a *source* and everything in creation ties back to that same intelligent source. Each individual chapter will be packed with an abundance of knowledge that is broken down, and each chapter is another step/level of understanding above the previous chapter you read before, creating a unique domino-like effect of understanding that can be retained more easily and for a longer time. The precise truth of who we truly are, who we truly were, and what all we can truly do as a massive consciousness has been the lifelong questions and an ancient mystery that has gone ages without ever being solved and answered, and it may continue to go unanswered and unsolved almost indefinitely. The truth of who we are has perplexed mankind for centuries, and hopefully, this book will inspire you to learn more about the unknown and at the same time also inspire you to apply this spiritual knowledge on your long destined journey of atonement and enlightenment. Whether you are a person who does not believe in anything at all or one who believes that there is a higher power that bent the natural forces to its will to create, which is perfectly fine either way.

On your journey of seeking the truth about creation and life, you will be led to one truth, see that everything is connected to that one truth, and then realize everything comes from that one truth. Some concepts within certain chapters won't be fully understood within a day. Some chapters you may even have to study and repeatedly read several times for it to sink in, and that is normal. Rome wasn't built in a day, but you can still continuously lay the foundation brick by brick. Even if you get through reading this book from cover to cover and you still don't believe one single word of anything that you read, by simply realizing and coming into the understanding or realization that everything in physical creation is interconnected will more than suffice. The information within this book is not meant to take known scientific concepts to explain spiritual texts, try to prove nor disprove the existence of what we call a higher power, nor try to explain away religious beliefs or traditions. Yes, we will dive into scientific concepts of each spiritual topic because it gives the student a reference point, something that is tangible that they can go and study themselves and use what they learned as a tool."

Providing something physical or that's relatable that the human brain can grasp easily makes complex information much easier to understand compared to someone just simply giving you abstract information with no reference points. The purpose of this book is to use information that most people don't already know exists and show the interconnected relationships between the spiritual world and the physical world, illustrating how we perceive things to be separate from each other when they are not. The second purpose is to simply demonstrate how all things in our physical existence have come from one individual intelligent source; regardless of whether you give that intelligent source a name or whatever name that source is given. Additionally, the book aims to demystify and shed light on those deep hidden spiritual truths and concepts in this age of misinformation.

A woman once asked the great Edgar Cayce how she could begin to expand her very own spiritual knowledge and overall spiritual awareness. He emphasized the need to compare the old ancient texts of other ancient cultures to expand our spiritual perspective, in accordance with the holistic principle stated in the Bible: there is only one God. There is only one cause for all of the effects we see and experience in creation. Most of us create our very own realities based on the things that we believe, and we reject anything that is different from our personal beliefs. Perception is not reality; it is simply only a filter through which we see. There is absolutely no religion that is greater or higher than the truth itself, and hopefully, the spiritual topics in this book will help lead you, the reader, to that one universal truth. Hold on! You're in for a ride!"

-Kevin S. Black

Introduction

What's Inside This Book?

In Chapter 1, We will begin to simplify the scientific understanding of **energy, frequency, and vibration** as well as to give simple examples to simplify each of their natural roles. We will also take a deeper look into the life of the great Nikola Tesla and get a better understanding of his unique role with energy

In Chapter 2, We will then extensively go over **9-Code** and how numbers have an influence on our physical reality. You will see how energy, frequency, and vibration is attached to numbers and how certain numbers are hidden in creation, nature and spiritual texts, as well as examine the Fibonacci Sequence and the Golden Ratio which will be the beginning of seeing creation being formed by "intelligent design" and how everything comes from source. You will also see how some of these same sacred numbers are hidden in the angles of specific shapes.

Chapter 3, Picks up where chapter two left off with shapes and explains the spiritual understanding of the **5 Platonic solids** and how these shapes are the basic construct for all matter in this three dimensional reality and how they assisted in the manifestation of matter. We will also dive into the secret ancient teachings of Sacred Geometry, as well as talk about the hidden energy centers spiraling in the human body that primary functions are to vitalize and balance both the physical and spiritual bodies known as Chakras. We will also discuss the function of Chi Energy and how it closely works with the chakra system in the human body.

Chapter 4, Dives a little deeper than chapter three and focuses more on the individual lines themselves that are drawn and bring into focus the way in which they were drawn. This will enlighten you and give insight on how drawing straight lines, *intersecting lines and geometric patterns* on paper or a surface generates and influences mystical forces and will cause spiritual phenomena to manifest within this three dimensional reality.

Chapter 5, intricately covers Entering into Other Dimensions and gives a very precise breakdown **of Space-Time** and **Time-Space**. We will also dive deeper and teach the difference between portals and wormholes and you will see that comprehensive and simplified examples will be given to explain dimensions and the functions of space-time and the time-space continuum.

Chapter 6, Touches on *Karmic Law and Reincarnation* and how the cycle of the soul fits perfectly into place with The Law of Grace and how these divine spiritual laws are a big part of divine order. I also will give Biblical scriptures as reference points

Chapter 7, Invites you to slowly drift back in time and learn about Past Life Regression. This ties into chapter 6 with **Reincarnation and Karma**. You will begin to see the hidden spiritual connections starting to take its form. We will also touch on in great detail what happens to our **Memories and Consciousness**, even go into **The Akashic Records** and will learn how the very universe itself has an infinite "Core" of stored information of every experience from every soul and event. Chapter 7 also dives into the extensive work of the man, the legend **Edgar Cayce** and his contribution to helping us understand The Akashic Records and the journey of the soul.

Chapter 8, Goes into depth and explains the difference between The *mind vs. the brain* and how it is the mind that works through the brain just as the soul works through the body. You will also meet an extraordinary woman by the name of Mary Ann Schinfield and her amazing extraordinary abilities. The magnitude of her gifts is way far beyond that of the average human being. One can say she has surpassed us all. Here is where we will also take a deeper look at human **Consciousness** itself.

Chapter 9, Dives into what exactly is *destiny and fate* and what is the difference between them. We'll also discuss how to take control of your own destiny. We also will talk about the power of our emotions, shaping our reality with intent/thought and the steps to invoke manifestation by learning how to sync thought with emotion to get the desires of the heart to manifest within a three dimensional space.

Chapter 10, Focuses on the ancient Hebrew, Greek, and English forms of what is known by the name *Gematria*. In mysticism, the hidden knowledge of gematria was very widely practiced amongst specific clandestine groups and those with higher education and knowledge throughout the mysterious ancient worlds and as well as the renaissance and medieval period to covertly hide the deeper esoteric meanings behind ancient spiritual text, including the Bible by ingeniously coding numbers in a specific way. This chapter will teach you how they used this technique and how you can apply it on your spiritual journey so that you too can get a much deeper and clearer insight rather than just stopping only at the literal or physical interpretations. The very same technique is used today in modern times to hide the deeper meaning of things.

Chapter 11, Is a very deep in depth and thorough breakdown on *crystals* and how their natural function influences people, objects, and the energies in its local environment. You will learn about their mysterious abilities and then we will greatly demystify their magical properties using known scientific research and data that you may not know exists.

Chapter 12, Shows how the earth itself generates its own natural energy and that energy then flows along invisible meridians or paths in straight lines we call **ley lines**. You will also see how these ley lines produce spiraling energy that we call **vortices**.

Chapter 13, We hear a lot about a person's aura and how it can affect others around us and even our environment. In this chapter, we will take a deeper look at **the human aura** and get a much deeper understanding of its natural function. We will also discuss the hidden interconnected roles of **the subtle bodies**.

Chapter 14, Are one of those topics we hear in every spiritual practice or esoteric circles. We will discuss what many people have experienced throughout the ages which, in modern times is identified as being an *Out Of Body Experience*, it is most formerly known in spiritual teachings as **Astral Projection**. We will discuss how our consciousness functions separately from the physical body and projects itself outward from the material body, working through the astral body/astral plane allowing for a much broader sense of spiritual awareness. We will also talk about the physical incarnating or the physical manifestation of the human Soul descending into the physical body.

Chapter 15, In this final chapter we pick back up on chapter eight diving deeper into the different levels of consciousness. You will learn about the different stages of **brain-waves** and how they affect not only us but the very fabric of physical reality when harnessed correctly. This chapter truly gives you a deeper insight into who you are as a spiritual being having a physical experience.

Table of Contents

Chapter 1: What is Energy, Frequency, and Vibration?? 1

Chapter 2: 9-CODE Energy In Numbers 13

Chapter 3: Sacred Geometry..26

Chapter 4: Aetheric Energy And The Power of Intersecting Lines .65

Chapter 5: Entering Other Dimensions; Space-Time vs. Time-Space..76

Chapter 6: Karmic Law and the Reincarnation of the Soul.............94

Chapter 7: Past Life Regression, Memory, and The Akashic Records 109

Chapter 8: The Mind vs. The Brain..122

Chapter 9: Destiny Vs. Fate 131

Chapter 10: Gematria & Numerology 141

Chapter 11: Crystals..152

Chapter 12: Ley-Lines and Vortices 165

Chapter 13: The Human Aura 173

Chapter 14: Astral Projection..192

Chapter 15: Becoming Supernatural; Attuning Ourselves to The Infinite 217

Afterword 229

Acknowledgments 231

Chapter 1: What is Energy, Frequency, and Vibration??

What is Energy, Frequency, and Vibration??

One of the greatest minds in history Nikola Tesla once famously said:

"If you want to find the secrets of the universe, think in terms of energy, frequency, and vibration."

Not only was Nikola Tesla known for his ingenious inventions but Tesla was indeed one of the first to realize the universe in its wholeness. We're not going to get too deep into the intricacies of energy, frequency, and vibration and their long list of spiritual functions in creation. However, I will give more simple definitions of these three incredible forces of nature with easy to understand examples so it will be easier to retain the knowledge especially if you are not familiar with the topic at hand in a particular chapter.

Vibration- is movement back and forth at a constant rate of speed over a specific period of time

Frequency- is the rate in which vibration occurs. Which is how we see sound-waves, radio waves, and the light spectrum when given the proper device? (This is simply measurement)

Energy- is the power derived from frequency/vibration. (the end-product of vibration.) It is an invisible field that envelops all things in creation.

To give a clearer example of these forces working in conjunction with everything God/*Source* created, look no further than the very first chapter of **Genesis** in the Bible. In the beginning it was a void, nothing, and out of nothing God moved upon the still waters and he began to speak things into physical existence. When we first read that scripture we truly missed out on maybe the most important information there is to know; both when God moved, and when he spoke. Both moving and speaking generates vibration, in turn frequency can be measured thus energy/power is the result.

At one point, our scientists believed that the smallest unit of matter in the entire universe was just a very simple molecule, but then discovered later on that the smallest unit of matter in existence is what we all now call an atom. After discovering the atom, another attempt to see what was smaller than the atom began to be widely explored. To the amazement of mainstream science, the only other thing that was and still is beyond the atom is nothing but spiraling energy. This was a very profound discovery because it seemed to correlate with the Bible; that everything came from energy and everything we know *is* in fact energy. Science and spirituality don't always agree, but the fact that this discovery coincides with texts over 2,000 years old is not simply by chance alone.

Biblically, we have witnessed how *Source* used energy, frequency, and vibration as his primary tools for all creation to completely influence the manifestation of our physical reality. Let me explain exactly what I mean when I say that both science and religion agree with each other. Just in the Bible alone, we see that Source moved upon the face of the deep, and then spoke physical material into existence. Moving is motion. Motion is vibration, and speaking itself is the vibration of the vocal cords or sound waves being generated, which therefore has a frequency and thus energy is derived and present. What is even more interesting is that everything is created and/or manifested out of energy, and we perceive that as being physical reality when physical reality doesn't truly exist in the way we believe it does. It may not make sense right now, but it will in later chapters when we discuss the behavior of the atom in the quantum realms and how this physical reality is affected by the immaterial world."

It's very important to note that all things in our existence have an energy, frequency, and vibration, therefore emitting an energy signature. There is nothing in this universe that is truly still, nothing at rest is truly at rest.

EXAMPLE: If you stand still in one spot for 24 hours

Did you move at any time during that time?

The answer to that question is yes, because

The earth has a planetary rotation.

The definition of motion is the action of moving

or being moved. When the earth rotates you are moving.

However, regardless if an object is moving are completely

still the object is moving because it has a vibration.

Everything in the universe vibrates.

Frequency is the rate at which a vibration occurs. It is the number of times a wave repeats or passes a fixed point in a given amount of time. So if the time it takes for a wave to pass or repeat is 1/2 second, the frequency is 2 cycles per second or simply 2 hertz. You can think of frequency as coded information that nature or all of creation deciphers as coded instructions to carry out a particular task or function to operate in a very specific manner. All frequency carries information because everything is in a state of vibration, no matter where on the spectrum it is. If you are new to this concept, just remember that (everything vibrates).

EXAMPLE: During the BP Gulf Oil spill in 2010. A scientist by the name of John Hutchison also nicknamed "The Mad Scientist" along with his longtime friend and associate Nancy Lazaryan, used 6,000 pounds of high military grade equipment to build this frequency generator to force the polluted water back into its natural frequency. By forcing water back into its natural frequency, you'll see almost like magic, **water will cleanse itself**. This is very ancient esoteric knowledge being utilized at its finest. Ancient knowledge displayed and utilized in modern application none the less.

During a national emergency response like the oil spilling into the ocean, a company called "Nalco Holding Company" which is a known subsidiary of "Ecolab." A trusted American water treatment and Purification Company were called upon to introduce a chemical dispersant and shoreline cleaner known as "*Corexit*" which at one point in time was originally created and developed by the Standard Oil Company. *Corexit* can be applied either by aerial spraying from military planes or by directly spraying onto the oil itself from ships. Once the chemical makes contact with the oil it then breaks down the oil into tiny droplets and it causes it to be suspended in the water by a process known as "**emulsion**." By purposely leaving the oil suspended in the water from emulsion, tiny micro-bacterial organisms naturally start to grow and take form and start breaking down the oil through another process known as "**bioremediation**." This chemical process combined with the frequency generator is how we saved our beautiful beaches and marshes.

Unlike the BP Gulf Oil Spill of **2010** where the Corexit and the frequency generator appeared to separate the oil from the ocean, we know energy, frequency and vibration cannot be separated. In fact separating these three components is nearly impossible. These three components work so close together in nature and throughout all of creation that if just one component was missing the physical and spiritual laws that govern three-dimensional space and time will fall apart and just cease to exist. If the atoms that make up your physical body as we discussed are made of energy and vibration and therefore have a frequency, just imagine for a moment if one of those components were missing. You couldn't begin to fathom what will happen to your body because the laws will then operate outside of three dimensional space and time. In order for frequency to be decoded and converted to information that can be understood and used, there at least has to be a receiver present that can receive the incoming signal and convert it to information that can be used.

Much like how a radio transmits a signal we call a broadcast, your radio or television receiver gets this coded information which is the incoming frequency and the radio or television then interprets the instructions and puts out the converted signal in a way in which your brain can interpret which is now either sound waves like the radio or both sound and picture like the television.

Well, nature has its own natural receiver. That is exactly why the grass knows to grow at a certain ratio, the seasons know when to come in, the sun knows when to rise and set, the moon influences the ocean tides etc. Everything in nature works in harmony and everything in nature is given an instruction you just have to be open to receive it and then, decode what you receive. Frequency is the number of times something (literally anything) happens in a given period of time.

$$frequency = \frac{1}{period} = \frac{(number\ of\ cycles)}{time}$$

[Figure 1.1]

If I jump on a bed **125** times in seven minutes or if I go to the bathroom six times in one hour, I have demonstrated frequency, which is the rate at which something occurs or is repeated per second, which now brings us to hertz.

Hertz or also sometimes referred to as cycles is the measurement of frequency. The Equation is represented as $f = 1 / T$. (F=

frequency, T= period) So if I jump on a bed 3 times in one second then I jump at 3 hertz or Hertz= 3/1 because remember its per second. So if frequency is the number of times it will take for something to happen, that means frequency is also the inverse (opposite) of the number of seconds it takes for something to happen. To put it simply, if you were to take 1 and divide it by the frequency you will get a measurement known as **period time**. As mentioned earlier, in physics, particularly in the study of waves, "period" refers to the time it takes for one complete cycle of a wave to pass a given point. The term "period" is denoted by the symbol T and is measured in seconds. It represents the time interval between successive peaks (or troughs) of a wave. Understanding the period of waves is crucial in various fields, including acoustics, optics, and electronics. It provides insights into the temporal characteristics of wave phenomena and is a key parameter in both analyzing and describing wave behavior.

Example 1: If a light bulb blinks 5 times per second

How long is the wait between each blink?

The frequency will be 5hertz because 5/1=5

and the wait between each blink will be 0.2 seconds

because 1/5=0.2

Example 2: If I go to the bathroom 6 times in one hour

(60/6=10) the period time is 10 minutes.

the time between each bathroom break.

Frequency = repeated patterns (f=1/T) Hz

Period = time between each repetition. (T=1/f) Sec

Knowing these equations can be fun and useful to have in your back pocket or your repertoire of memory when learning about frequency but don't get lost in the math and miss the experience. A lot of times we will see numbers and start to shy away from what can potentially be an amazing learning experience. Nikola Tesla once said:

"The day science begins to study non-physical phenomena; it will make more progress in one decade than in all the previous centuries of its existence".

How Tesla saw the universe was light-years ahead of his time and his existence is still continuously contributing to humanity almost 100 years later. After all, his nickname was "The man who invented the 20th century." We owe the discovery of Wi-Fi to NikolaTesla. He figured out that electricity can travel wirelessly and was determined to push mankind forward.

Who was Nikola Tesla

Nikola Tesla was born July 10th 1856 in a small hometown village in Smiljan, Croatia. In 1884 Tesla came to the United States with only four cents in his pocket, a few of his poems, and calculations for a flying machine. With a letter of recommendation he landed his first job working at Thomas Edison's laboratory. Edison was known for his direct current (D.C)

Direct current, (DC) while Tesla was known for alternating current (AC). In Edison's way of using electrical current it flowed only in one direction and lost energy over long distances, while Tesla's method was a type of electrical current, in which the direction of the flow of electrons switches back and forth at regular intervals or cycles. To put it more simply, here is an easy example of the two methods:

Flashlights, and other devices used to store power for charging like our phones and laptops will be Edison's method. Power running through your home in multiple directions will be Tesla's method. Another example is if you had two houses with all the lights turned on in both, one house will be running off of Direct current (Edison's method) and the other house will be running off of Alternating Current (Tesla's method). If you would turn off one switch in Edison's house then all the lights in the house will turn off because the current is flowing in one direction, but if you turned one switch off in Nikola Tesla's house, then just that one room light will turn off. Tesla's method was not only much more efficient but it was also very convenient. This characteristic made AC the preferred choice for electricity distribution over large geographical areas, facilitating the creation of extensive power grids. The work of Nikola Tesla, a pioneer in AC technology, played a pivotal role in demonstrating its advantages. AC's ability to be easily transformed between high and low voltages made it easily adaptable for various applications, from powering homes and industries to facilitating the development of electric motors.

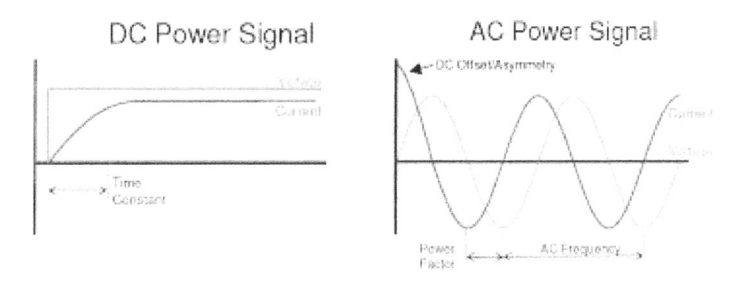

[Figure 1.2]

Tesla's Method was more efficient because electricity traveled over long distances with minimal energy lost and without having to put a power plant every few miles unlike we see with Edison's method. The letter of recommendation Tesla carried to the U.S in 1884 was from a mutual friend of Edison's and when he opened it, it read *"I know two great men. You are one of them, and the other is this young man"* and Edison gave Tesla a job. One evening, Edison had installed a bunch of DC dynamo's (convert mechanical rotation into electric power) on a large ship called SS Oregon (as shown in Figure 1.3). Suddenly all of the generators malfunctioned and there wasn't anyone on the ship that could figure out why, not even Edison himself. So, Edison assigned the task to the young 28 year old immigrant Tesla. Tesla stayed up and worked all through the night until finally, he had restored functionality to all of the dynamos and Edison praised him as a "Damn good man". Tesla fully believed that his alternating current invention that he spent years developing can help and give Edison's design more efficiency and lower the cost it takes to build. Edison said "If you can do this young man, it will be worth $50,000 to you". So with very high hopes of getting this large sum of money to put towards his inventions and a new lab, Tesla worked vigorously until he upgraded Edison's dc design. When Tesla approached Edison about the money Edison told Tesla that he didn't understand American humor. At that very moment Tesla resigned. In 1893 there was an exposition that took place at the Chicago world fair. Nikola Tesla, along with business partner George Westinghouse, had unveiled their alternating current to the world. Inventors were invited to submit bids to light the fair using electricity. In the lead of course were Tesla and Edison which will later be known as "Battle of the Currents." Edison submitted a large bid for $554,000 using his D/C method But George Westinghouse, armed with Tesla's patents for A/C power, bid $399,000 and won the contract. Tesla used neon fluorescent light bulbs and lit up the entire fair. It was the most amazing thing people have ever seen.

In 1895, Tesla and well known industrialist George Westinghouse had created the world's very first hydroelectric power plant at Niagara Falls. A huge competition was then held to see who can generate power over long distances between Tesla and Edison. The Tesla power plant generated power from Niagara Falls all the way to Buffalo, New York without having power plants every few miles, and because of this, alternating current was the system chosen to power the world.

[Figure 1.3]

In November of **1900**, Nikola Tesla caught the attention of financier J.P. Morgan. Morgan signed a contract with Tesla in **March 1901**, agreeing to give the inventor **$150,000** to both develop and build a wireless station on Long Island, New York that would have the capability of sending wireless messages to London as well as ships at sea. Also written within the contract was Morgan having a **51%** interest into the company as well as a **51%** share in present and future wireless patents developed from the project. Tesla had a new and determined rival named Marconi who was transmitting radio signals beyond the range of what was believed to be impossible. Marconi was actually sending radio waves miles over the horizon which led Tesla to believe that Marconi was using his Tesla coil to achieve this using his famous earth resonance method. Tesla went to J.P. Morgan asking for more money to build something else even better and more advanced that was different from what was agreed upon in the original contract and J.P. Morgan refused. Sadly in 1943 while in a New York hotel room the brilliant Nikola Tesla was murdered. He was found dead from coronary thrombosis, which is a blockage of the arteries supplying blood to the heart, leading to a heart attack with his safe emptied and his research and briefcase missing. Tesla's forward-thinking inventions and bold ideas have continued to influence modern technology and culture, shaping the way we live today. His work has left not just a legacy but a passion that still burns in the hearts of young aspiring engineers of today. His work will continue to advance for hundreds of years to come.

[Figure 1.4] Nikola Tesla

Chapter 2:
9-CODE
Energy In Numbers

We've learned that frequency instructs nature, telling it when to move, how to move, and even how long to precisely sustain something. No one has to step outside of their doors to tell the four seasons when to come in. No one says, 'Hey Spring, it's time to make the weather warm,' or has to tell those beautiful autumn leaves to simply drop from their branches in the fall, or even have to go out of their way to tell the snow that it's time to sleet snowflakes in the winter time. This is precisely done, in large part, by what is known in very small mystic and secret society circles as the 9-Code, a divine system of geometry ingeniously created and hidden that is so perfectly entangled into the fabric of our reality. One must understand that numbers themselves truly contain energy. All of nature simply follows these instructions because of frequency, and frequency has very code-specific instructions that are encoded into itself, and of course vibration. Frequency in nature can carry either one or a multitude of complex code-specific instructions.

In order to fully understand just how numbers influence reality, it will be easier to show you examples that are in creation. God's creation was, and still is, based solely upon divine mathematical laws that both govern and influence everything in physical creation, both in the physical world and non-physical world. It is still, to this very day, penetrating and still permeating through all the multi-dimensions beyond space and time. So, in order for you to truly get a solid fundamental understanding of just how numbers hold power and energy, I will move from Bible scriptures as well as from a science and numerology perspective. In that moment, you will begin to see that divine intelligence is the genius architect of the universe."

Romans 1:20, NIV:*"For since the creation of the world God's invisible qualities--his eternal power and divine nature--have been clearly seen, being understood from what has been made, so that people are without excuse."*

In this scripture Paul is telling us that there are things that are in fact knowable about God and creation but why when some of us look at creation we don't see God or a divine intelligence behind it? Well, the answer is in the verse before.

Romans 1:18, NIV: *"The wrath of God is being revealed from heaven against all the godlessness and wickedness of people who suppress the truth by their wickedness"*

Here, Paul is telling us that we don't see the entire truth because we continuously engage in low vibratory activities that constantly blind us from the truth, and we don't genuinely seek to gain true wisdom and understanding. The things that are knowable about creation and life are just waiting to be discovered, but they will not reveal their secrets if we still operate in a low vibratory state. In other words, if we consistently put our physical bodies in a low vibratory state of being, we are inadvertently suppressing all access to much necessary, vital, and infinite knowledge and wisdom. This mainly is because we are unknowingly not connecting ourselves to *Source* so there will inevitably remain to be a disconnect between mankind and the *Source* of all things. Let's try to look at it from this perspective. In order for us as true seekers of knowledge and followers of Christ to understand the knowable secrets of creation, have them revealed to us, and then manifest, our desired frequency has to match the frequency of the intent that already exists in the quantum or unified field. Meaning, your thoughts and desires work hand-in-hand. When done properly, your thoughts and emotions are in complete coherence, you will turn your body into a magnet.

Once you have the thought [mind] of wanting to know more and having access to more knowledge of creation, you will then realize that once you begin to properly align that thought, [mind] with your desire/emotion, [body] then mind and body will become one and the body becomes like a magnet drawing in any desire or intention. The more you subject yourself to the unified field the more and the easier it is to be aware of hidden esoteric information that we walk through on a consistent basis, but more on manifestation in a later chapter. It doesn't matter what faith that you practice. If you are genuinely searching to find truth, wisdom and understanding from an honest place in your heart then you will attract truth, wisdom and understanding. Hopefully that little nugget has opened your mind and heart to receive. Now, let's get back to the numbers. Think of numbers' role in creation like this.

When you use a cellphone, you dial specific numbers, and that's because those specific numbers influence specific frequencies so if you want to call "John Doe" you will have to instruct the phone exactly who to call by inputting numbers in a very specific sequence or combination. In turn, that specific frequency dialed which is an (instruction) now gets sent to John Doe's phone. The instructions that you had just dialed or inputted on the keypad were specific instructions to make John Doe's phone ring which will notify John that you're trying to reach him. Now once you have input the instructions to make the call to that specific person's phone, it takes energy for those frequencies to travel from point A to point B and all frequencies carry energy, and all frequencies carry information.

Now that you understand that numbers carry energy and that all frequencies carry information, now I think it's time to dive into the numbers. Nikola Tesla had once told us that one of the keys to us understanding the universe is to understand the numbers 3, 6, and 9. Everything in the universe breaks down to 9 and therefore 6, then

3 because 9 and 6 are divisible by 3 and 3 divide into itself once. The number 9 appears in the Bible 49 times and symbolizes finality of God's creations and his promises. Edison, a blog writer over at *Lifecodes*, gives us the perfect examples of 9-Code as seen on the following page.

9code In The Bible

- Jesus died at the 9th hour, which was 3 p.m.
- Jesus appeared 9 times to his apostles after resurrection.
- There are also 9 spiritual gifts of God.
- The last king of Israel, Hoshea, reigned for 9 years.
- Number 9 is also known in the Bible as the number of judgment.
- Day of Atonement on the 9th day of the 7th Hebrew month.
- There are 9 fruits that are mentioned in the Bible and some of them are goodness, gentleness, etc.
- August 9th was the day of the destruction of the temple in Jerusalem.
- Herod's temple was burned by the Romans August 9th
- There are 9 generations from Adam to Noah.
- Abraham was 99 when he got his name.
- 666 (6+6+6=18) (1+8=9)

9code In Creation

- Diameter of the moon= 2,160 miles (2+1+6+0=9)
- Speed of light travels 186,624 miles per second (1+8+6+6+2+4=27) (2+7=9)

- Diameter of the moon is 2160 miles (2+1+6+0=9)
- Diameter of the earth is 7920 miles (7+9+2+0=18)(1+8=9)
- Diameter of the sun is 864,000 miles (8+6+4=18)(1+8=9)
- The first four digits of *PI* π = 3.141(3+1+4+1=9)

Note: The speed of light in meters per second is (29.9792458) and the speed of light is also hidden within The Great Pyramid of Giza which is located at (**29.9792458**) degrees north latitude. The speed of light is **299,792,458** in meters per second and the diameter of the earth is (**7920**) and is also hidden inside of the speed of light as **792** (**7+9+2=18**)(**1+8=9**). We also use the first four numbers in *PI* π = **3.141(3+1+4+1=9)**.

The size of the earth, the speed of light and the distance from the sun to the earth cannot be coincidence at all. The reason being, is because the universe itself was created by intelligent design; and if one intelligent *Source* is behind all of this and is still, in complete control of every single outcome of every single moment in our existence, then that would mean that coincidence itself cannot exist nor co-exist alongside *Source*. It is also key to point out that we didn't create math, we only re-discovered it.

If you bisect circle in 2 parts **180(1+8=9)**

If you bisect circle in 4 parts **90(9+0=9)**

In 8 parts **45(4+5=9)**

If you bisect circle in 16 parts **22.5(2+2+5=9)**

In 32 parts **11.25 (1+1+2+5=9)**

In 64 parts **5.625 (5+6+2+5=18) (1+8=9)**

In 64 parts **5.625(5+6+2+5=18)(1+8=9)**

The resulting angle always reduces to 9.

60*3=180 (1+8=9) circumscribed circle of a triangle

4*90=360, (3+6=9) is the circumscribed circle of a square.

108*5=540, (5+4=9) circumscribed circle of a Pentagon.

120*6=720, (7+2=9) circumscribed circle of a hexagon.

135*8=1080, (1+0+8+0=9) circumscribed circle of an octagon

More Facts About Nine

- nine plus any other digit will return back to the very same digit **9+2=11(1+1=2) or 9+5=14(1+4=5)**
- The total sum of all the other digits without using the nine is **36 (1+2+3+4+5+6+7+8=36) (3+6=9)**

Number 9 and It's Correlation To Time

There is exactly 1440 minutes in a day **(1+4+4+0=9)**

86400 seconds a day **(8+6+4+0+0=1800) = (1+8+0+0=9)**

There are 10080 minutes in a week **(1+0+0+8+0=9)**

525600 minutes in a year **(5+2+6+0+0=18) = (1+8=9)**

[Figure 2.0]

Fibonacci Sequence and The Golden Ratio (phi)

The Fibonacci sequence is a set of numbers that starts with a one or a zero, followed by a one, and proceeds based on the rule that each number called a (Fibonacci sequence) is very much equal to the sum of the preceding two numbers. As shown, each number equals the sum of the two numbers before it. If you take a look at [figure 2.3] you will see how the next number value in the sequence is generated. The Fibonacci sequence is repeatedly found everyday throughout nature, and the ratios associated with those numbers. So where does the Golden Ratio or Phi come into play? Well both in nature and in architecture, we see that if you have a straight line and divide it into two parts for example, the long part divided by the short part and the whole length divided by the long part you will get Φ1.618 which is the golden ratio. As my teacher Ms. Flake used to tell us in geometry, the length of A+B equals the total distance of C. Or more simply (A+B=C). Life itself is geometry hidden in the pockets of reality, the sacred tool that created all life on Earth.

Think of it this way, if you look closely at [figure 2.4] you will see that the curve continuously oscillates going over and under the straight line not quite hitting dead on and never meeting the straight line flat lining in the center. As a quick side note, straight lines do not occur in nature no matter how much it looks like it or how much we want them to and Phi is a major part of that .As the curve lines get shorter and shorter, it gets closer and closer to meeting the straight line every time getting closer and closer to phi but never quite hitting it. Now since phi in decimal form **(1.6180339)** is an irrational number it goes on forever. Soon the curve will become so small that you won't even be able to see it and tell if it ever flat-lines. It never does. It will continue to go on coming close to phi but never hitting its mark. When nature decides to follow and move toward the Fibonacci Sequence or the golden ratio design, everything in nature flourishes and strives to create and grow as close to perfection as possible. To put it simply, Source is infinite and eternal and doesn't have a beginning and doesn't have an end, so *Source* decides to create everything in existence and then instructs nature to continue to create. Now unlike *Source*, nature isn't eternal or infinite. A flower seed isn't exactly eternal nor is it infinite, so that flower seed must start from a beginning or have a starting point, so it starts at one, thus creating the Fibonacci sequence. As that flower seed grow to become an individual flower, the seed will continuously hit ratios or numbers that are within the Fibonacci sequence every time bringing the seed closer and closer to perfection, moving closer and closer to *Source*.

[Figure 2.1]

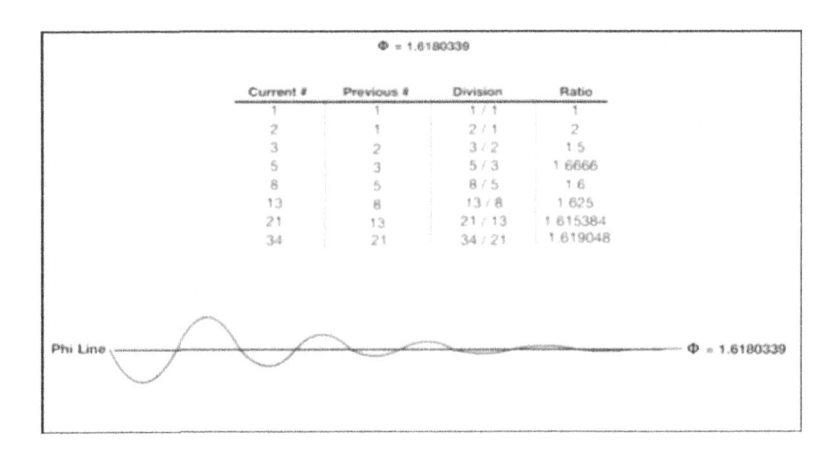

Current #	Previous #	Division	Ratio
1	1	1 / 1	1
2	1	2 / 1	2
3	2	3 / 2	1.5
5	3	5 / 3	1.6666
8	5	8 / 5	1.6
13	8	13 / 8	1.625
21	13	21 / 13	1.615384
34	21	34 / 21	1.619048

$\Phi = 1.6180339$

[Figure 2.2]

This sequence is then broken down into a ratio. The Fibonacci sequence is significant because of the (golden ratio) sometimes called the golden mean of 1.618 or its inverse 0.618. Discovered within the Fibonacci sequence is any given number approximately 1.618 times the preceding number ignoring the first few numbers. Each number is also 0.618 of the number to the right of it, again ignoring the first few numbers in the sequence. Again, the Golden ratio or "phi" is the ratio of a line segment cut into two pieces of different lengths such that the ratio of the whole segment to that of the longer segment is equal to the ratio of the longer segment to the shorter segment. You don't have to remember all of this and get lost in the math. Take a look around you in nature and all creation and just get lost in such a majestic experience. Just take a look at how it appears throughout nature and art in the images in this chapter. Beauty is the expression of the overall underlying unity, harmony, and divine order of the cosmos. The Golden Ratio also symbolizes spiritual evolution and the journey of the soul. Just as the Fibonacci sequence and the Golden Ratio are present in the spiral growth of plants and shells, they are seen as metaphors for the evolution of consciousness—a spiral ascent from the lower to the higher levels of awareness. The spiral represents the unfolding of life, not in a straight line but in a dynamic, ever-expanding pattern of growth

Fibonacci Sequence

0, 1, 1, 2, 3, 5, 8, 13, 21, 34, 55, 89, 144, 233, 377, 610, 987 …

Each number is the sum of the previous two numbers.

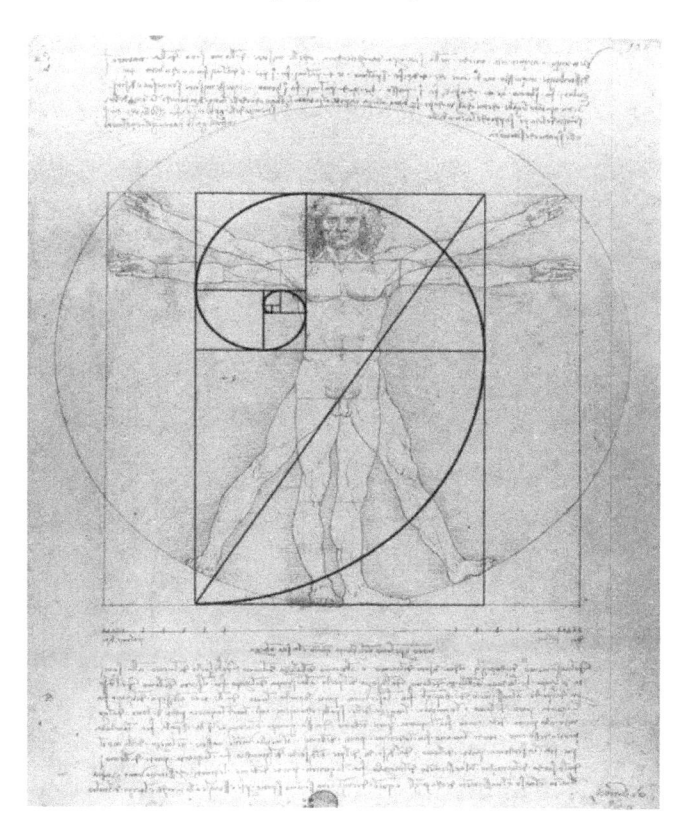

[Figure 2.3]

[Figure 2.4] Leonardo Davinci's Vitruvian Man

[Figure 2.5]

[Figure 2.6]

In many ways life itself is a computer simulation. We all are inside of a matrix. **Revelation chapter 13 verse 18** clearly states that if one has wisdom and understanding to count the number of the beast, which is also the number of a man, then he will find that his number is **666. (13x18=234) 2+3+4=9**. **234** plus its opposite **432** is also **9 (4+3+2=9)**. There are hidden numbers that constantly appear in creation and they are **9, 11, 12, 24, 72, 234, 432, and 864**. If you have at least somewhat of a basic understanding of simple math you will instantly notice that all the numbers are associated with nine. Either they are divisible by **3** or by adding the two digits the sum will equal nine. However, if math wasn't your favorite subject in school you may take a closer look at the number 11 and you will ask yourself how is this connected to nine when neither it is divisible by three nor do either of its digits sum to nine? The number nine and eleven are always near each other, just as **9** and **6**, which are upside down of each other to form a vortex shape. Example, If you divide:

100/9 = 11.1111111111. And **100/11** you get **9.090909090909**.

Where nine is, eleven isn't too far behind and vice versa. If you look at a calendar you will notice that September is the 9th month yet uses the prefix Sept which also means **7** in Latin. The month of November is the 11th month and uses the prefix Nov, which means 9. Even the days of the week themselves are planets in Latin. Sunday is the day of the sun, Monday is the moon day, Tuesday is Martes which is Mars, Wednesday is Miercoles which is Mercury, Thursday is Jueves which is Jupiter, Friday is Viernes which is Venus and of course we know that Saturday is Saturn. You are in the Matrix Mr. Anderson. From an esoteric perspective, many old traditions and philosophies hold that numbers do indeed govern reality, serving as the fundamental principles that shape both the material and spiritual worlds. Numbers are seen as more than mere abstract concepts or tools for measurement; they are considered the underlying fabric of existence, carrying symbolic, metaphysical, and cosmic significance.

[Figure 2.7]

Chapter 3:
Sacred Geometry

What is Sacred Geometry?

Sacred Geometry is an ancient science taught in mystic circles that explains the energy patterns that create and unify all things in creation as well as to ascribe symbolic and sacred meanings to certain geometric shapes. A **platonic solid** is a regular polyhedron in which all the faces are the same and each face meets at each vertex. There are only five platonic solids or platonic (shapes) in physical existence and they are the following: The Tetrahedron, Hexahedron, Dodecahedron, Octahedron, and last but certainly not least the Icosahedron. These five Platonic solids got their infamous names from the world renowned Greek philosopher Plato himself. Though these mysterious shapes themselves have always been in existence and named after the great Greek philosopher, the use and knowledge of these shapes and the power in these shapes were known only to those within esoteric circles. This is one of my favorite subjects. First, before we go further. I would like to say that this is a very deep topic that goes far beyond and outside the scope of average human thought processing. Some of what is in this chapter will not make sense as a whole until you read further into the chapter and your mind will begin to put the pieces together; and only then will you eventually see the pieces beginning to take shape. Don't worry, we won't fully go too far down this rabbit hole of sacred geometry because the information is just simply way too complex and the very basics itself is complicated enough but however, you will still have enough of the information to see just how energy, vibrations, harmonics, music and even matter are all interrelated and have been since the dawn of creation. Sacred

Geometry was once taught in the most prestige's mystic schools and was widely understood as universal truth.

SACRED GEOMETRY 5 ELEMENTS
PLATONIC SOLIDS

TETRAHEDRON - FIRE
HEXAHEDRON - EARTH
OCTAHEDRON - AIR
DODECAHEDRON - AETHER
ICOSAHEDRON - WATER

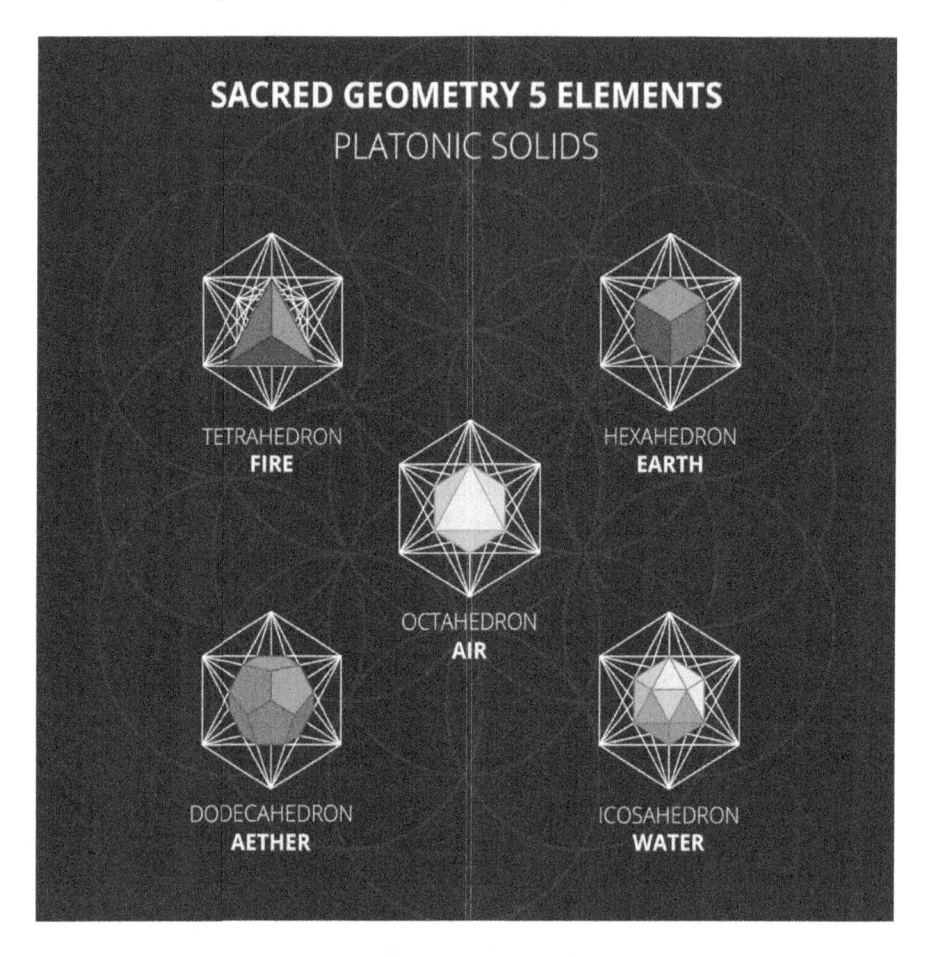

[Figure 3.1]

These five shapes are the basic fundamental structures that make up all things in physical and non-physical existence. In 360 B.C Greek philosopher Plato theorized that these five platonic solids represent the five elements. Plato believed that these solids were not just physical representations of the elements but reflected the geometrical order that underpinned reality itself. For him, geometry and mathematics were the keys to understanding the universe, as they had represented the ideal forms—unchanging, perfect, and eternal—which, in his theory of forms, were the true reality behind the imperfect material world.

- Hexahedron or the (Cube) represents EARTH/Reconnecting to nature.
- Octahedron represents AIR/Compassion.
- Tetrahedron represents FIRE/Balance and Stability.
- Icosahedron represents WATER/Enhanced thought and Expression.
- Dodecahedron represents AETHER or ETHER/Mysticism and meditation.

Plato wasn't the first to discover the 5 platonic solids but is credited with its discovery because not only of *whom* he was and the title he had in

Mysticism often interprets the five Platonic solids—regular convex polyhedra with identical faces, angles, and vertices—in symbolic and a lot of spiritual ways. Here's a brief overview of the mystical interpretations:

Tetrahedron (Fire): The tetrahedron, is a sacred shape with its four equilateral triangular faces, is often associated with the element of fire. It represents transformation, energy, and spiritual awakening. Some mystics see the tetrahedron as a symbol of the divine spark within each individual.

Hexahedron or Cube (Earth): The cube, with its six square faces, is closely linked to the element of earth itself. It symbolizes balance, stability, material manifestation, and the physical world. Mystics may interpret the cube as a representation of the structured and grounded aspects of reality.

Octahedron (Air): The octahedron, which has eight total equilateral triangular faces, is closely associated with the element of air. It is often seen as being a symbol of harmony, and spiritual evolution.

The octahedron is thought to facilitate the integration of opposing forces.

Dodecahedron (Aether/Universe): The infamous dodecahedron, with its twelve regular pentagonal faces, it is sometimes associated with the fifth element we call aether or quintessence. This shape is considered to be a representation of the whole universe, cosmic order, and its divine consciousness. It is believed to symbolize the integration of all other elements and the connection between the microcosm and macrocosm.

Icosahedron (Water): The icosahedron, with its twenty equilateral triangular faces, is associated with the element of water. It is often linked to emotions, intuition, and the subconscious. Some mystics interpret the icosahedron as a symbol of flow, adaptability, and the ever-changing nature of reality.

In mystical traditions, the Platonic solids are sometimes used as meditation tools or symbols to help individuals connect with higher consciousness, explore hidden spiritual concepts, and understand the underlying unity of our very existence. It's important to note that interpretations can vary among the different mystical traditions and society belief systems, but because of his in-depth knowledge and understanding of something that was so very complex, it led to him connecting these shapes back to Source and creation. In ***Timaeus***, Plato wrote and gave precise mathematical formulas constituting each of the platonic solids formed from right triangles which lead to his "Theory of Everything." The most sacred and mystical shape of all the platonic solids is the Dodecahedron. Plato once said that God/Source used this shape for the entire universe. An example of this is in the Ley-Lines. [Figure 3.2] Though we don't yet possess the technology to see these lines we have proved they are there by drawing straight lines from all the ancient sites from across the world, and we know that the earth's magnetic field is strong along those lines. The idea of an energy grid is often connected to sacred geometry, which posits that the universe and all of creation are governed by geometric patterns and mathematical ratios.

We see these five shapes appear in:

- Cytology
- Chemistry
- Astrology
- Geology
- Meteorology
- Mineralogy
- Medical Virology and Psychological Perception.

These five solids are unique in that they have the same number of faces meeting at each vertex, the same angles between faces, and they are the only regular polyhedra. Their symmetrical properties have fascinated most mathematicians and philosophers throughout history, and they hold symbolic significance in various spiritual and mystical traditions. The study of Platonic solids is foundational in geometry and has many connections to broader philosophical and metaphysical discussions about the nature of reality. Renowned for their mathematical elegance and symmetry, these solids have fascinated scholars and hold symbolic significance in philosophy, spirituality, and various ancient traditions. The Platonic solids were, in Plato's view, perfect expressions of cosmic harmony and order, reflecting the ideal geometrical forms that structure the material world. Plato believed that the cosmos was created with a sense of proportion and balance, and these five shapes mirrored that divine order. The dodecahedron, with its connection to the universe, also hints at Plato's belief in a cosmic soul or a divine mind that created and governs the universe. He suggested that the universe itself has a kind of intelligence and that the shapes found in nature reflect a deeper cosmic truth, created according to hidden mathematical and geometrical laws. Plato's ideas about the Platonic solids have had a significant influence on esoteric and mystical traditions throughout human history. In later metaphysical thought, these five solids were seen as powerful symbols of creation, the primary building blocks of both the physical and the spiritual realms. This lead us to ley-lines.

[Figure 3.2]

The earth has known **ley-lines** or energy paths that run through it both latitudinal and longitudinal which creates and is known as "Earth's Energy Grid." We now have the technology to see this amazing energy grid and the grid is indeed in the shape of the Dodecahedron. This mysterious shape was so sacred that if you were caught just whispering its name outside of the Pythagorean Mystic School you were killed. These five very powerful shapes whether seen in honeycombs, in seashells or in the formation of a fertilized egg like observed in cytology have mystical power and influence over nature and can also easily influence matter which we'll discuss later. If you look at [figure 3.3] this image has been seen in almost every religion on earth and drawn the very same way. It is the universal symbol of creation. In fact, no matter where you travel in the world it is called by the same name, The Flower of Life. The Flower of Life is considered to be hidden knowledge due to its historical presence in ancient cultural sites symbolizing sacred geometry and the interconnectedness of life. It also holds hidden esoteric wisdom about creation, consciousness, and the universe, fostering a sense of mystery and spiritual significance.

Roger Green, founder of Academy Of Sacred Geometry says that

"It is a pathway to understanding who you are, where you are from and where you are going."

[Figure 3.2]

When talking about Sacred Geometry there are a few things that you will hear constantly and that is: **The Seed Of Life, The Egg Of Life, The Flower Of Life, The Fruit Of Life, The Tree Of Life**, and **The 5 Platonic Solids**. The Seed of Life also called **The Genesis Pattern** is exactly what it sounds like. All things created both in the material and the non-material world comes out of one geometric pattern which is the Seed of Life. There are too many things that exist in creation to just name them all entirely however; *emotions, thoughts, musical notes, every possible known and unknown mathematical formula, the secrets behind the ancient pyramids, mysticism, magic, alchemy, the periodic table etc.* are just some, but yet not limited to just one system of information. Literally every single tangible and intangible thing comes out of one singular pattern and that pattern is the blueprint and the key to the universe and also the key to mankind understanding the universe or multiverse as a whole. Everything there is to know about the flower of life cannot be put all in one chapter. In fact an entire book will have to be written and dedicated to just the discoveries of the flower of life alone, and that one book still wouldn't be enough for one individual to fully understand the flower of life. If we were to dive deep into every single information system in existence and connect how each and every individual system ties back to the Source of all things, most people will not make it past the first chapter because it is just simply way too much information to try to completely understand just from reading one complete chapter, and therefore discouraging the reader from continuing their study.

Instead, I will make it as simple as I can to show enough proof to the point that you will be encouraged to further your study all on your own. The truth is, just watching or reading about the flower of life you are only getting a very small fraction of knowledge about creation and the world around you, but if you start drawing the patterns yourself you will see even more things that connect back to source and you will be amazed as to where the knowledge and new found understanding will lead you. The seed of life, The egg of life, The fruit of Life, The tree of life, The flower of life, The 5 platonic solids All come out of a system known as Sacred Geometry. In the beginning of this chapter it starts with the definition of what exactly is Sacred Geometry. Now let's take a look of what that definition actually means and how exactly it applies to God himself and all of creation. Sacred geometry is an ancient and spiritual practice that explores the inherent mathematical and sacred geometric principles believed to underlie the creation of the universe. It involves studying specific geometric shapes, such as the Flower of Life, Metatron's Cube, and the golden ratio, which are all considered symbolic and representative of divine proportions. Practitioners often associate sacred geometry with mysticism, spirituality, and a deep connection between the physical and spiritual the realms.

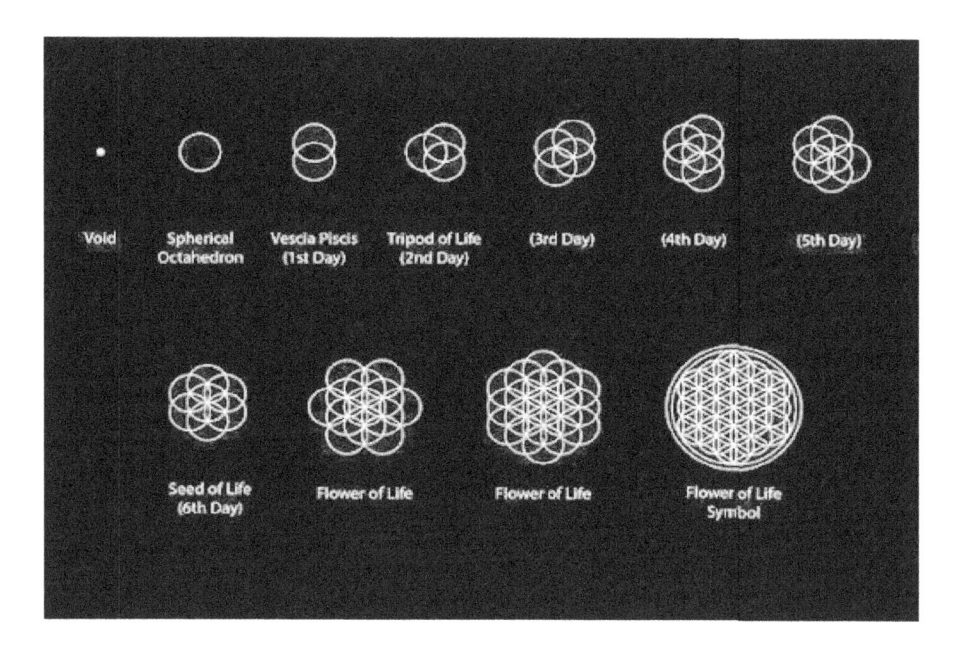

[Figure 3.4]   Marcel Vogel

If you look at the diagram in [Figure 3.4] Mystic Researcher Marcel Vogel Have created an excellent representation to help visualize the creation story in Genesis. Make sure from here on to read very slowly, even go back and reread just to make sure you understand it because studying the flower of life can be confusing.

In the beginning there was a void [figure 3.4] and the earth and everything in the universe was without form. Physical matter wasn't created yet. So, the first dot that you see in the diagram is Source [God], or you can call *Spirit*. Now *Spirit* is inside of a void so *Spirit* just hovers or floats because there is absolutely nothing to move in relation to and motion or kinetic energy doesn't exist yet. There is no up, there is no down, there is no left, and there is no right. It's just a void. Spirit decides that it wants to create so the first thing spirit does is project its very own consciousness in all directions all around itself creating the first sphere that you see in [Figure 3.4.] Now with this awareness inside of the void motion or kinetic energy is possible because now there is something to move in relation to inside the void. It is spirit's own consciousness that allows the movement or motion to be possible and so now spirit can begin to create inside of this empty void. I think it is safe to say that the first thing created in physical existence is sound, motion/vibration because everything in this world vibrates so therefore everything has a sound regardless if you can hear it. Now Spirit creates this sphere around itself, next Genesis 1 says that he moved upon the face of the waters. This is the first day as shown in [Figure 3.4]

Day 1 Spirit is perfect so when spirit moves, spirit moves in perfect movements. So the spirit perfectly moves 1 radius in any direction to the edge of the sphere and projects its consciousness again creating 2 Spheres. Now it is here we see in the center of this sphere, it creates a fish shape we see a lot in Christianity called the **Vesica Pisces** as shown in [Figure 3.5] and [3.6]. It is here the first system of information will manifest itself into physical reality.

How? Well, because inside of the Vesica Pisces is an abundance of infinite knowledge of width, ratios, proportions, square root of $\sqrt{2}$, $\sqrt{5}$ and $\sqrt{3}$ the list goes on and on. So much knowledge was released and used during the very first day of creation it's impossible to go through all of it because there is just way too much to go into, let alone fully comprehending it all. There are some researchers and metaphysical thinkers that .believe that the Flower of Life contains the blueprint for our DNA. The pattern's structure mirrors the double helix of DNA, suggesting that it reflects the fundamental structure of biological life. This has led to the idea that the Flower of Life is the key to understanding how life itself is encoded. The interwoven, spiraling pattern of the Flower of Life contains this same twisting geometry when viewed three-dimensionally. If you look deeper into the molecular structure of our DNA, it's composed of nucleotides arranged in specific patterns. The sugar-phosphate backbone of DNA forms a hexagonal structure, which can be mapped onto the hexagonal shapes that arise from the circles of the Flower of Life.

Here are a few Flower of Life examples of the Vesica Pisces and its connection the Bible.

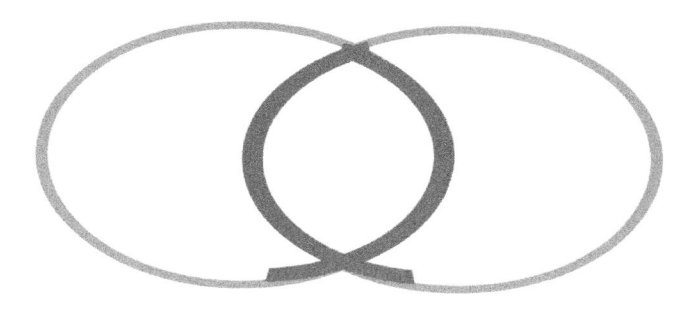

[Figure 3.5]

[Figure 3.6]

John 21:

⁶ And he said unto them, Cast the net on the right side of the ship, and ye shall find. They cast therefore, and now they were not able to draw it for the multitude of fishes.

⁷ Therefore that disciple whom Jesus loved saith unto Peter, It is the Lord. Now when Simon Peter heard that it was the Lord, he girt his fisher's coat unto him, (for he was naked,) and did cast himself into the sea.

⁸ And the other disciples came in a little ship; (for they were not far from land, but as it were two hundred cubits,) dragging the net with fishes.

⁹ As soon then as they were come to land, they saw a fire of coals there, and fish laid thereon, and bread.

¹⁰ Jesus saith unto them, Bring of the fish which ye have now caught.

¹¹ Simon Peter went up, and drew the net to land full of great fishes, an hundred and fifty and three: and for all there were so many, yet was not the net broken.

The focus of this scripture is the **153** fish and the deeper meaning of what it actually represents in relation to the Vesica Pisces and the first day of creation. If you make the intersection of two circles a height of **265**, the width will equal **153**. 153 represent the width of the Vesica Pisces. The mathematical ratio of the height of the Vesica Pisces to the width **(153)** across its center is the square root of **3** or **1.732**. In other words **254** divided by **153** is **1.732** which is the square root of **3** in decimal form. [See figure 3.5.] On the first day of creation spirit just didn't create mathematical proportions, but light as well.

If we take the name *Mary Magdalene* and translate her name to Greek, it becomes η αγδαληνή. A name that we couldn't even begin to pronounce with our North American linguistic system. If we add the numerical values to each letter and then add those values together the result will come out to be **153**. Even the names of some of the biblical figures had a deeper secret meaning behind them. In **Genesis 1** we see that in the beginning God created the heavens and the earth And the earth was without form, and void; and darkness was upon the face of the deep. And the Spirit of God **moved** upon the face of the waters. And God said, Let there be **light**: and there was light.

If you were to simply follow the first few scriptures up until creation was complete, and then correspond each day with each individual sphere as seen in [Figure 3.4], you will see the connections in your mind's eye. If you look closer to the words that are bold you will see there were two things that took place the very first day of creation. Out of nothingness, God **Moved**, creating the second sphere, then came **Light,** which its mathematical components are within the Vesica Pisces.

Also, the square root of three or $\sqrt{3}$ is exactly the length of the diagonal of a cube. In other words, this simply means because the structure of the cube is in a three dimensional shape then a three dimensional space or reality therefore can be defined. That alone is just simply amazing. Everything you interact with everyday is three dimensional this world, this life we call reality is three dimensional and therefore can be defined see [Figure3.7] The square root of two or $\sqrt{2}$, was the math used in building Solomon's Temple, and the square root of five or $\sqrt{5}$, is what appears within the Golden Ratio, which means it's very sacred and appears all throughout nature and creation and it is part of a universal law. The very idea that numbers such as $\sqrt{2}$, $\sqrt{3}$, and $\sqrt{5}$ are not just abstract mathematical concepts but the very principles that guided the creation and very structure of reality itself gives us greater insight into the hidden interconnections between mathematics, nature, and spirituality. Let's look at day two.

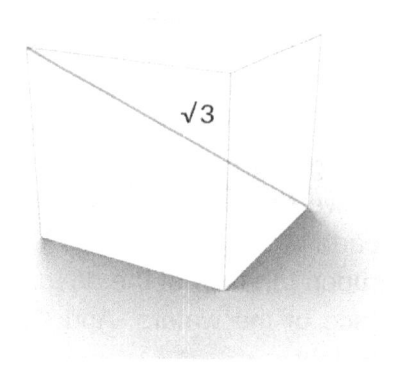

[Figure 3.7]

Day 2 Spirit again, moves perfectly, moving exactly one radius away in another direction to the edge of the last sphere and does the exact same thing that it had just done before. Spirit projects its consciousness thus creating a third sphere. Now this third sphere creates the Holy Trinity or a shape known as the **Triquetra**. The Triquetra has been used by first century Christians to symbolize the Holy Trinity and unity. As you will come to learn in a later chapter most religious symbols you see today do not belong to any specific culture or religion but instead have existed long before the creation of any religion and even man itself. Shapes and the mathematical proportions of those sacred shapes already existed. The Triquetra has been seen in sacred Indian sites over 5,000 years old, Northern Europe, on the early Germanic coins, and yes even in forms of witchcraft like Wicca. **On October 7, 1998** one of the greatest shows of all time which happens to be one of my favorites, was aired and it was called **"Charmed."** A story about three sister witches who had the sacred triquetra symbol inscribed on their spell book. [See figure 3.8.] Religious symbols predate the creation of any formal religion. These symbols are archetypal representations of universal truths that have always existed in the fabric of reality. The cross, the Star of David, the ankh, the yin-yang, and others are not creations of human civilization but are manifestations of cosmic patterns, sacred geometry, and universal laws that have been present since the beginning of time

[Figure 3.8]

Day 3-5 more spheres of consciousness are projected which in turn means an abundance of more information is added each day. This is why I said that when studying the flower of life it is impossible to put it all in one book and one book by itself still wouldn't suffice. There is simply way too much information to be discovered in one lifetime and to be all understood in one lifetime. Keep referring back to [figure 3.4] to see the spheres being created if it gets confusing.

Day 6 This is where something amazing reveals itself. During this final day of creation the spheres make the shape of what is called and known around the world as **The Seed of Life.** Within all 6 spheres is nothing but secret knowledge and wisdom of our creation. Every time spirit moved, spirit encoded a vast amount of secret knowledge about life and creation into the fabric of reality for us to find. this makes me think of Deuteronomy.

Deuteronomy 29:29

The secret things belong unto the LORD our God: but those things which are revealed belong unto us and to our children forever, that we may do all the words of this law.

When you genuinely search for truth and seek out the creator of all things, there will be secrets that will be revealed to you, knowledge that no one else around you possess. These secrets are not revealed or given to those who are not seeking truth or trying to get to source and align themselves with source. So when those secrets of life and the secrets of creation are revealed through source it is our job to make sure we pass that information down to our children and the people around us. I got a little off track but let's get back to the subject matter at hand. **The Seed Of Life** also known as **(The Genesis Pattern)** as seen in [figure 3.9] has another unique hidden shape within it which in sacred geometry and what the mystic teachings call **The Egg of Life** as seen in [Figure 3.10.1]

If you see the hidden connections with the spheres and the book of Genesis then you will see why The Seed of Life is also called the Genesis pattern. Now you are about to see why The Egg of Life is hidden inside The Seed of Life and why it's called The Egg of Life. The Egg of Life get its name because in biology it is the shape seen in cell division where the original 8 cells through a process known as *meiosis*, doubles itself as it expands. Take a closer look at [figure 3.11.2] from Flower of Life researcher Celeah Norris.

Celeah Norris is a spiritual artist and reknown author known for her deep exploration of the interconnectedness of the universe, with a very particular focus on the "Flower of Life" symbol and its deeper meanings. Her spiritual work spans across various artistic mediums, including sculpture, and often delves into themes of astronomy, geography, and human consciousness. Through her art, she seeks to understand the relationship between human existence and the cosmos. One of her main interests is sacred geometry.

[Figure 3.9]

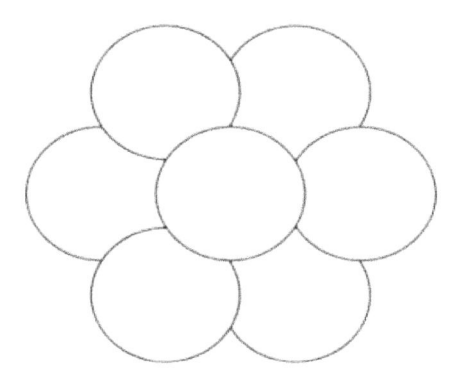

[Figure 3.10]

[Figure 3.11]　　　blogs.uoregon.edu　　　Celeah Norris

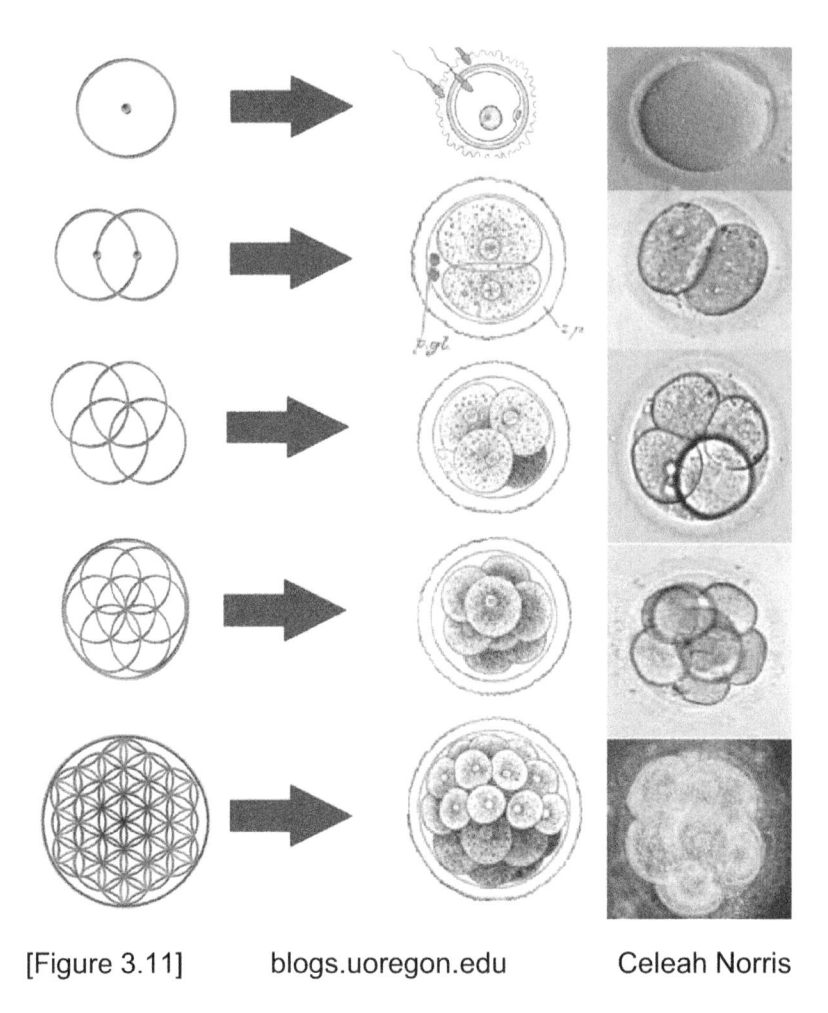

What also comes out of the flower of life is the Tree of Life which can be seen in the kabbalah practice, (Jewish Mysticism) which is a discipline or a very sacred esoteric method used for interpreting and understanding the deeper hidden esoteric truths or meanings within spiritual text. The Fruit of Life can also be seen hidden within the flower of life. The Fruit of Life is exactly what its name insist. It is the fruit. It is the *result* that contains the fine details of the fabric of our reality and everything in existence.

THE FLOWER OF LIFE

EGG OF LIFE   SEED OF LIFE   FRUIT OF LIFE

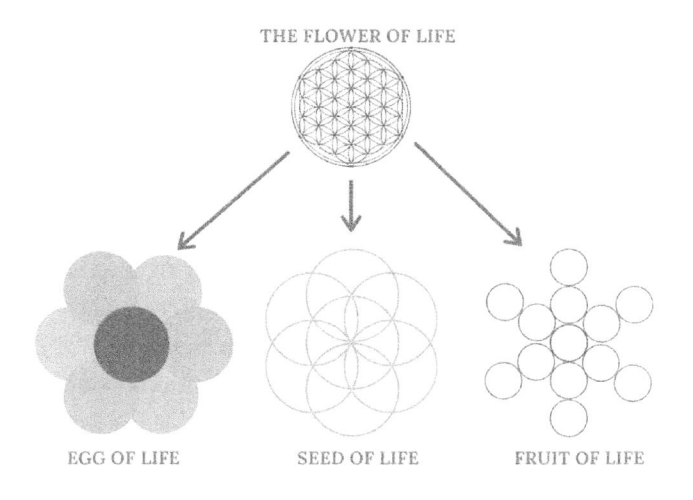

[Figure 3.12]

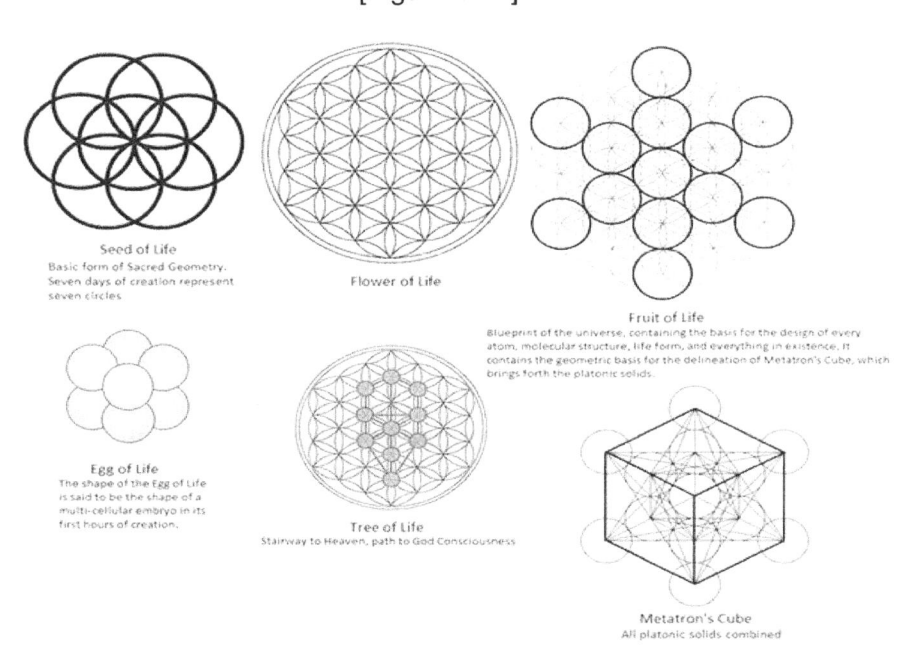

Seed of Life
Basic form of Sacred Geometry.
Seven days of creation represent
seven circles

Flower of Life

Fruit of Life
Blueprint of the universe, containing the basis for the design of every
atom, molecular structure, life form, and everything in existence. It
contains the geometric basis for the delineation of Metatron's Cube, which
brings forth the platonic solids.

Egg of Life
The shape of the Egg of Life
is said to be the shape of a
multi-cellular embryo in its
first hours of creation.

Tree of Life
Stairway to Heaven, path to God Consciousness

Metatron's Cube
All platonic solids combined

[Figure 3.13]   Image from SymbolSage.com

There are two things that is key to remember when speaking or studying Sacred Geometry, That is curves and circles represent female energy and straight lines represent male energy. It's easier to remember when thinking about human anatomy. Women waist tends to be more curved than men's, while men waist tends to be straighter than women's. So what in the world does this have to do with anything you may ask? Well, if the Fruit of Life contains the knowledge of everything within the fabric of this reality, and if we look at The Fruit of Life a little closer, we will see that it consist of circles, nothing but female energy. Now, watch what happens when we combine male energy with female energy. When we take The Fruit of Life and draw straight lines from the center from every circle to every other circle, it will create what is known throughout the universe and every esoteric circle as **Metatron's Cube.**

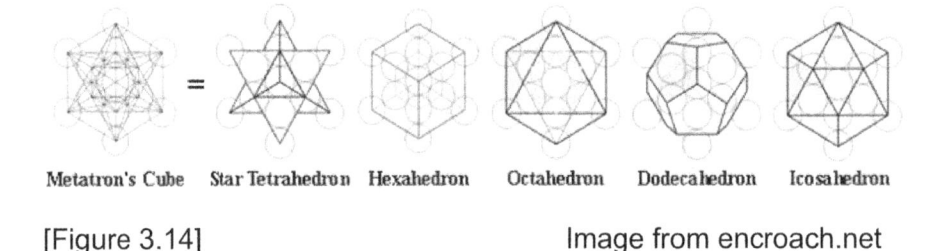

Metatron's Cube   Star Tetrahedron   Hexahedron   Octahedron   Dodecahedron   Icosahedron

[Figure 3.14]   Image from encroach.net

If I had to simplify the spiritual meaning of what Sacred Geometry is, it can be more easily understood as being the whole of creation. I would say that it can be looked at from a broader perspective of *Source*/God using a very sacred or hidden form of geometry that manifest infinite repeated geometric patterns that conjures the vibrations, sounds, harmonics, music, and matter that is needed for the creation of physical and non-physical life, everything included from the seen to the unseen conjured into the fabric of reality, and then unify all those things within that reality. Sacred Geometry and the five platonic solids also play a very significant role in our body's

45

energy field and our chakra system. The deeper you study into the primordial energies of creation you will at some point realize that every single thing that makes up every fiber of your entire being is connected back to the universe directly; and since you are part of the universe and everything in the universe is connected to *Source*, then you come from *Source*.

Chakras And Chi Energy

What are Chakras? Chakra comes from the ancient Sanskrit word meaning "wheel" or "disk" and they are spiraling wheels or vortexes of energy that are located in specific locations in the human body. **Chi has** various names in every culture. In China it is called **Chi** or **Qi**. In Japan it is called **Ki**. In India it is called **Prana**. In Buddhism it is called **Virya** and the Hawaiian's call it **Mana**. No matter the name, its very function is still all the same. It is the living life force energy that permeates throughout all living and nonliving things. So what exactly is the difference between Chi and Chakra? First, this book is unbiased, so to be completely fair, I just want to say that there is no definitive scientific evidence of chi and chakras or any device known to be created for it to ever be proven [Indefinitely]. So with that being said, chi energy and chakra both work together inside the human body's energy system. Those of us that practice martial arts or various forms of other spiritual practices or meditation have had our very own mystical or spiritual experiences outside the realm of what any man-made scientific instrument can measure or test. Note that within the very well respected field of Quantum Mechanics, created as a branch in the early 1920's, to this present day, is still filled with theories trying to explain the physical properties of nature at the atomic and subatomic levels that have yet to be proven. This means that for the last 100 years alone we have been basing our lives off of theories of things which cannot be explained and have yet to be proven. Scientists refuse to believe what can't be tested or experienced with the five basic senses or inside a laboratory. As of right now in this time there is no scientific tool or device that has been invented as of yet that we know of, that allows us to see, definitively test, or even physically experience spiritual or mystical experiences or phenomena outside of this three dimensional reality. [Not including E.V.P] [Electronic Voice Phenomenon.] My humble advice to any person that is studying mysticism or any spiritual practitioners that is exercising their faith or practice, is to continue walking on your path of enlightenment and atonement and keep doing what you have been called to do. One day science will catch up to what some of us already know.

Root Chakra   *Sacral Chakra*   *Heart Chakra*   *Throat Chakra*   *Third Eye*   *Crown Chakra*
Basic Trust   Sexuality/Creativity   Love, Healing   Communication   Awareness   Spirituality

[Figure 3.15]

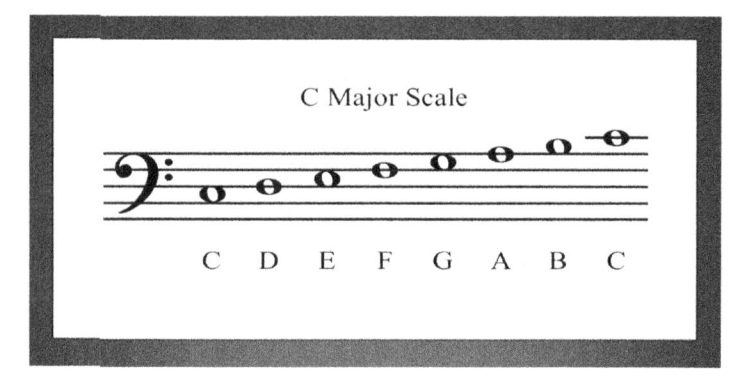

[Figure 3.16]

The difference between Chi and Chakra is that Chi is the living life force energy that seamlessly flows in and out and all around all living and nonliving things. In fact you can think of it as what Star Wars calls "The Force." Chi is located two to three inches below the belly button inside of the abdominal muscle which some in the east called the *Dan Tien* at the base of the spine and is the storehouse and primary energy center of the human body. [Its location will make sense later] Chi also can be manipulated by a person who is trained properly and Chi comes in various forms. For the sake of simplicity and understanding I will only be referring to the Chi within the human body. Chi is Life force energy. Think about the last time you seen a sick, hurt, helpless animal caught in a trap that just been severely injured by a very hungry predator, or maybe even you have experienced a family member or friend that are on their sick bed just slowly drifting, fading out of this world because cancer won't loosen its deadly grip around your loved one. Think back to those vulnerable moments or that specific moment you experienced that feeling. In those kinds of situations it's almost as if you can feel their life force, their spiritual energy fading away. You can sense that their very essence is about to disappear. If you take a look back at [figure 3.15] and then take another look at [figure 3.16] you will then notice that the music notes on the scale follows the same frequency patterns as the chakra frequencies within the human body.

That is what **Chi** is. All living things have a life force and that life force is passed down to our children every time a woman bears a child. Almost like a domino effect. God/Source not only gave us the Breath Of Life that runs through our bodies, but what we never think about is that same life force energy itself which is very much closely related and interconnected to oxygen or the Breath Of Life, the life force energy is so sacred because source gave it to Adam, from there Adam became a living soul. Source only shared it with one individual and every time a person is born that life force energy is shared into a newborn's body at every single birth as well as with oxygen. An infinite supply of life force energy all from giving it to one person once is incredible. I slightly got off topic but hey, I digress. Hopefully, there is one thing you will soon come to realize throughout this entire book, and that is how vital every small detail is.

Chi has a very important role in our overall vitality and daily lives. Whether we choose to notice this or not is solely up to the individual person to come to that conclusion for themselves. The chakra network itself is equally important and without the chakras our life force or *Chi* energy wouldn't flow properly and can end up causing a lot of serious internal organ damage and even cause death. Chakras are an invisible gateway if you will, in which Chi flows through corresponding to the bundles of nerves, major organs, and other unique spiritual areas of our energetic bodies that affect us physically, emotionally and spiritually. Each chakra point; if you ever notice is always associated with a color and always has that same color associated with that specific chakra no matter where you are in the world. These same exact colors correspond to musical notes on a scale. There is a reason for that which also will be explained later. Just take a closer look at the figures below for a more visual understanding of the chakras.

[Figure 3.17]

[Figure 3.18]

[Figure3.19]

[Figure 3.20]

[Figure 3.20.1]

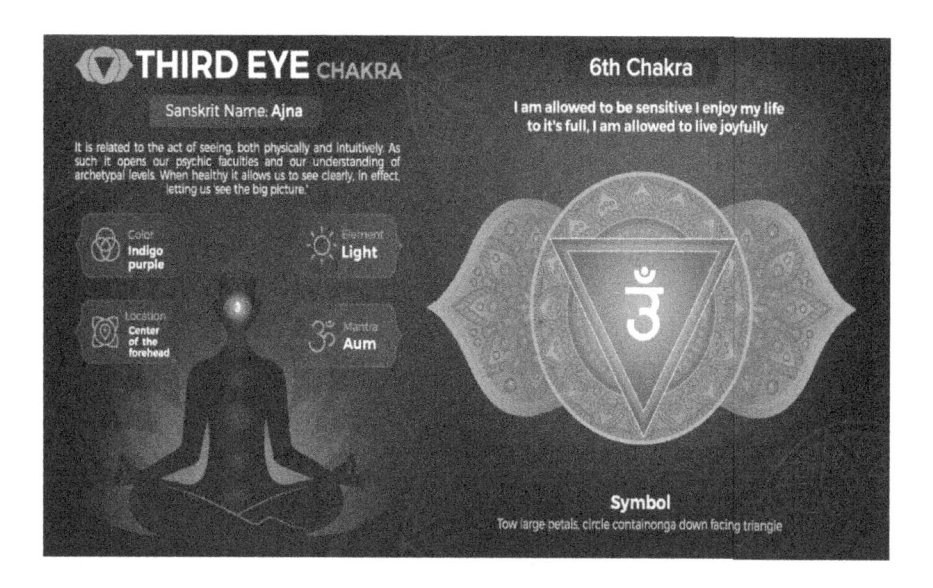

[Figure 3.20.2]

[Figure 3.20.3]

Earlier I had mentioned that Chi or Life Force Energy is stored and housed two to three inches below the belly button/navel inside the abdominal muscle sitting at the base of the spine. That may sound confusing and a bunch of mumbo jumbo but just follow me and it will all make sense to you. By now you realized that all of the chakras run up alongside the spine. There is a very good reason for that. You will see here shortly the spine itself has a hidden purpose that was implemented in our anatomy by *Source* since the very beginning of our creation. There are a total of one hundred fourteen known chakras in the body. However, there are seven primary chakras that have become popularized and what most people know of and these seven chakras are the chakras that run along the spine. Let's simplistically break down the connection between the belly button and the spine first. Each segment of your spine is a single vertebra. It is entirely composed of thirty-three bones which make up the spinal column. Follow so far

From there, the spine is then broken down even further into the five different known sections. They are as follows: **Cervical**, **Thoracic**, **Lumbar**, **Sacral**, and **Coccyx**. We're not going to go into detail into each and every one, but the one with the hidden purpose that ties into spiritual awareness and awakening is the **Lumbar**. The lumbar includes the five vertebrae that make up the lower curve of our spines' just behind our belly button. That is no coincidence. Here we see that the base of the spine lines up exactly in line with the belly button which is the store house of Chi or life force energy. What is also very important to know is that the **spinal cord** runs along the inside of the vertebral column. The spinal cord has a key purpose. The base or the lower part of the brain is connected to the spinal cord. Which is why together, the brain and spinal cord are known as the central nervous system.

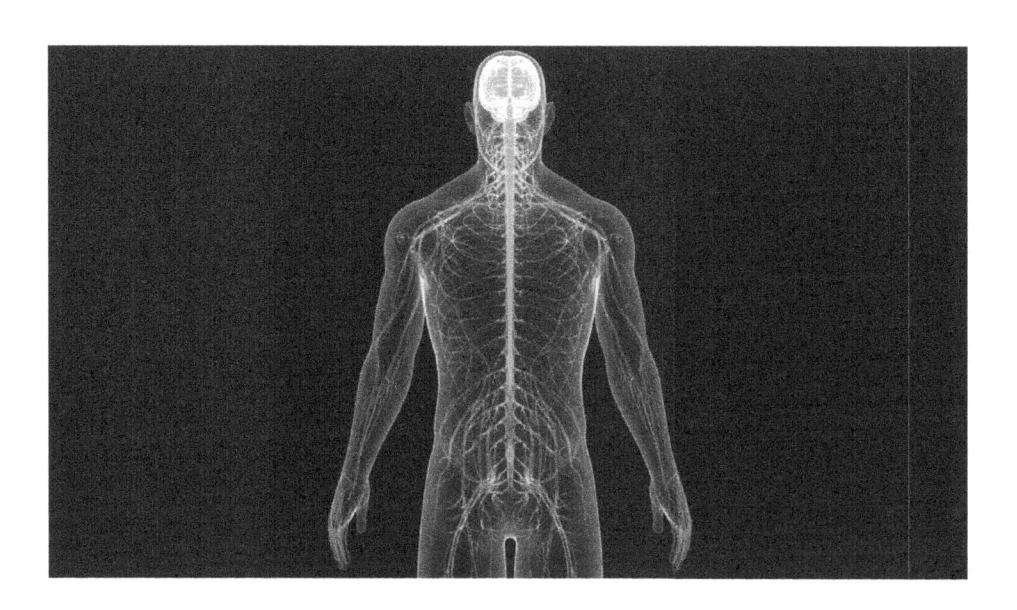

[Figure 3.20.4]

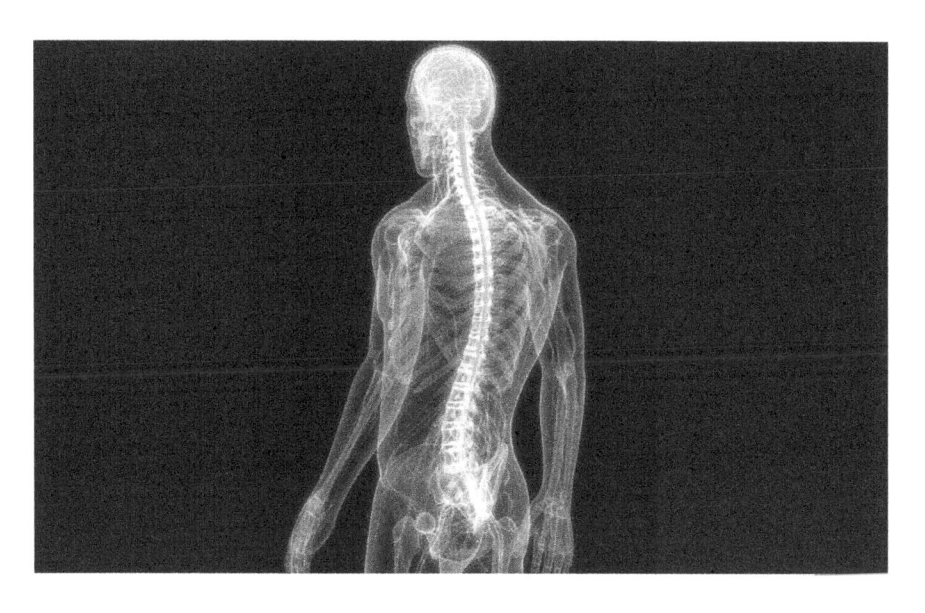

[Figure 3.20.4]

Here is why your spinal cord and spine are important. The spine itself protects the spinal cord because the primary function and focus of the spinal cord are to act as a communication conduit. Information literally flows through your spinal cord. Its purpose is to transmit and receive information. Remember in the earlier chapters when we had learned that all energy carries vast information? Well, therefore all information has energy, frequency, and vibration. Here is where all of it begins to connect. The medical terminology for the belly button is umbilicus. Your umbilicus connects to the fibers that lead straight to the spinal cord, like a socket connecting to this invisible conduit of information. The brain and spinal cord are your body's central nervous system. The brain is the command center for your body, and the spinal cord is the pathway for messages sent by the brain to the rest of the body and from the body back to the brain. The transmitting and receiving of information inside the spinal cord can be understood more simply like this:

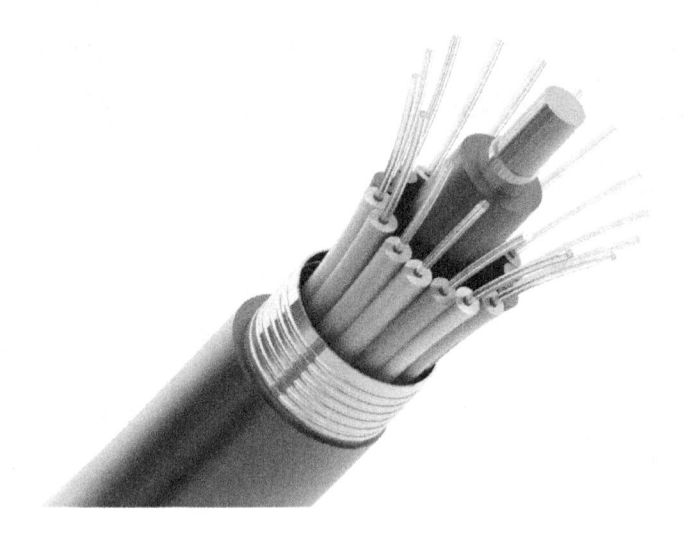

[Figure 3.20.6]

If you take a closer look at [figure 3.20.6] you will see that is what we all call a fiber optic cable or an optic fiber. It is a recently new technology used and seen implemented in the manufacturing of our cars, homes to even being implemented in Wi-Fi routers. Fiber optic cables work similarly to how the information is transmitted and received in the spinal cord. Unlike old traditional household power chords that carry electrical current, optic fibers carry or transmit and receive information/data in the form of light back and forth from one end to the other. Exactly the same way the information in the spinal cord flows. Earlier I had mentioned that each individual Chakra is associated with a specific color and no matter where you go in the world the association of that color to that specific chakra will never change and the colors will always be in order from the lowest frequency all the way up to the highest frequency. For Example, growing up in elementary and middle school at some point we were all taught the colors of the rainbow. More specifically some of us, not all of us, were taught the colors of the rainbow in precise order, from bottom to top we remember to this very day and still see the acronym in our children's classrooms, R.O.Y.G.B.I.V

Red, Orange, Yellow, Green, Blue, Indigo, Violent. The reason the colors are in order is because Red vibrates at the lowest frequency and as you go up to the next corresponding color it vibrates at a frequency much higher than the color before it. If you look back at [figure 3.14] you will see that each chakra is associated with the same colors of the rainbow and each chakra shares the same frequency as that individual color. So what does the colors of the rainbow and the same colors associated with those specific chakras themselves have to do with the chakras being in specific locations in the body? Well, what that tells you is that each organ or area close to that specific chakra point operates on or around that specific frequency for vitality and optimal performance. So for example let's throw a random number out there and let's say the Liver operates or vibrates at a frequency of 65 Hertz. In order to keep my liver healthy I better make sure that I keep my liver at or around 65 Hertz at all times.

I want to make it perfectly clear that the chakras themselves don't have or make energy but again, work as gateways for our chi energy to work through. To explain it simply, think of chi energy as life force energy that disperses itself throughout the body giving all your major and minor organs life and vitality. Now think of meridians like energy rivers or a stream in the human body that flow in various directions. The body naturally has these invisible energy lines that pass through vital organs and various places throughout the body. Chi or life force energy flows along these invisible streams similar to how a pebble will get carried in a river. The precise points at where these meridians or energy streams/rivers intersect are called chakra points. Now the chi or your life force energy will naturally follow the path or flow of these meridians, so once the flow of your chi energy travels to one of these chakras or energy centers which acts as a gateway, and that gateway is blocked, [usually by some kind of emotion] then that chi energy gets stuck and can't continue to flow to the next gateway or to the next chakra energy center until the individual completely deals with that emotional distress. Sometimes our emotions can act as very large boulders in a stream or river and sit at these gateways or energy centers and thus preventing and blocking the natural and seamless flow of our own life force energy. These blockages can cause unexplained sicknesses or even death. Once that emotional distress or those negative thoughts have been dealt with by the individual and then completely removed from that particular energetic center, then the chi energy can then continue to seamlessly flow to the next gateway or energy center.

Every time the chi energy moves up to the next chakra energy center, the vibration of your mind, body, and spirit then rises to a much faster and higher frequency. Therefore, once you begin to vibrate at a faster or higher frequency or wavelength, you will tap into an infinite consciousness and you will be plugged into universal consciousness. Now that you understand all the information that was just discussed, let's dive just a little deeper and talk about what exactly happens when all the chakras are open and what happens when Chi Energy makes its way all the way up into the crown chakra.

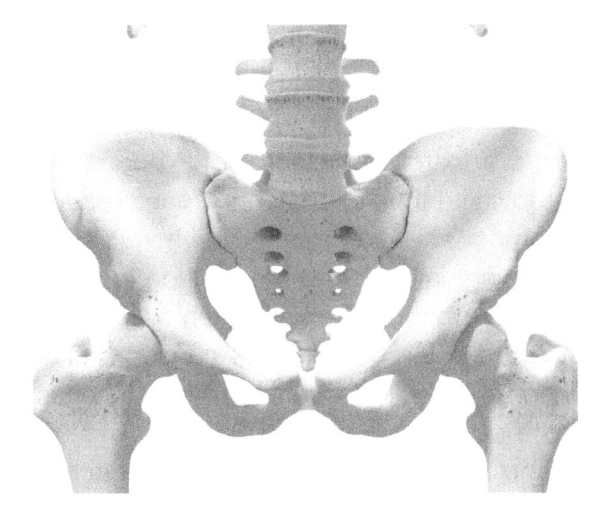

[Figure 3.20.7]

Spinal fluid seamlessly moves in various directions, following various paths, delivering nutrients, chemicals, and other necessities of bodily functions up and down the spinal cord from the skull to the base of the spine constantly. Here is how Chakra infused with Chi Energy through meditation can lead to mystical and unexplained spiritual experiences during meditation. At the base of the spine is the sacrum bone, which extends all the way to the skull and looks exactly like an upside-down triangle [Figure 3.20.7]. Every time we inhale and exhale, the sacrum slightly moves backward and forward. This movement is so slight that you wouldn't even notice it even if all of your attention were focused on it. According to Dr. Joe Dispenza in his book "Becoming Supernatural," there is what we call the **Cranial Sutures** on the skull. Basically, the skull has a mechanism that acts as an expansion joint that slightly opens and closes, connecting and disconnecting like a puzzle piece, giving it a little elasticity in very small movements, and it only occurs in the skull. This allows the bone to enlarge and expand evenly as the brain grows and the skull expands. Most of our human skulls are not fully fused at birth, which is normal but fuses as we get older. Again, this only occurs in the skull. During childbirth, the flexibility of these sutures allows the bones to overlap so that the newborn's skull can more easily pass through the birth canal without pressing on and damaging their brain [See Figure 3.20.8].

Cranial sutures are extremely essential for normal skull and brain development, providing the flexibility and space required for growth. They serve an important role in infancy, where the brain is rapidly expanding, and eventually fuse to create the protective structure of the adult skull. Any abnormalities in suture development, such as premature fusion, can lead to medical concerns and may require treatment. When an infant has spent too much time just lying in one position long, the skull can develop a flat spot. This can occur if the cranial sutures do not allow for even expansion across the skull. It is generally treated by repositioning the baby or using a special helmet.

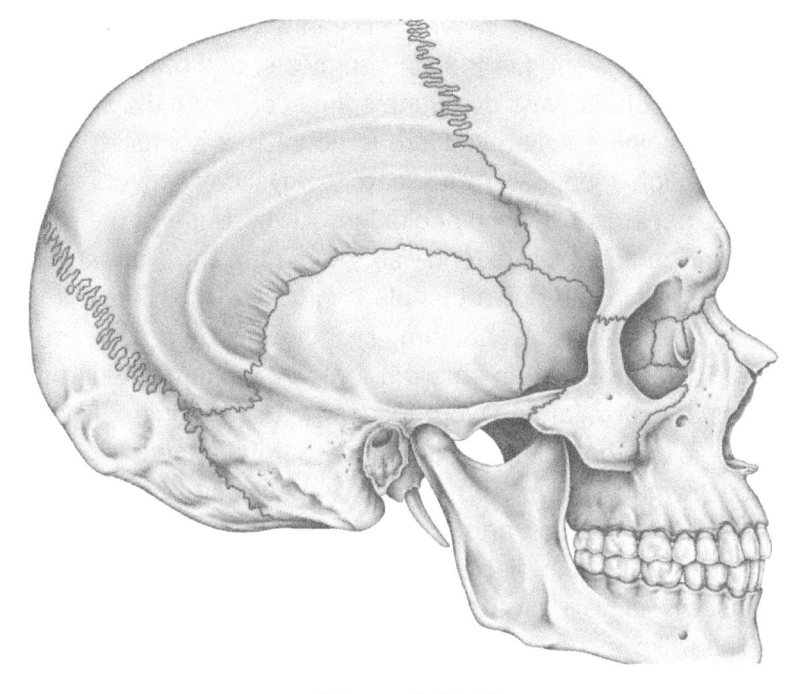

[Figure 3.20.8]

Now back to the sacrum bone. As stated above, both the sacrum and the sutures constantly move. If you understand this correctly, then yes, at the same time you inhale, the sacrum slightly moves backward and slightly opens the sutures in the skull, and when you exhale, the sacrum slightly starts moving forward and sutures on the skull close back again. In other words, every single time that you breathe, your skull is constantly opening and closing. It is this movement of the sacrum, combined with the movement of your skull opening and closing from your slow inhaling and exhaling, that incites the spinal fluid and slowly pumps that fluid up the spine along the chakra energy centers into the brain. According to Dr. Dispenza, the brain bathes in spinal fluid constantly. One of the major factors to entering that heightened state of awareness or the beginning of entering into infinite consciousness is to accelerate the spinal fluid by purposely forcing it up the spine into the brain. You may be thinking this information is irrelevant, and what does spinal fluid have to do with the energy centers. In fact, spinal fluid has a hidden secret and here is what it is. Cerebrospinal fluid is made of proteins and salts that are in a solution.

When the proteins and salts begin to dissolve in a solution the molecules that are inside of the proteins and salts then become charged particles. Any time that you take a charged particle and accelerate it like forcing the proteins and salts up into the spine you will create what is known in science as an **inductance field** as shown in [Figure 3.20.9], which is an invisible electromagnetic field that moves in a toroidal motion in the same direction the charged molecules or particles are moving in. The more you accelerate the charged particles the stronger the inductance field becomes. When you activate your chi energy at the base of the spine, now this female energy creates what is known as a **Kundalini Awakening.** It's female energy because it doesn't move in a straight line; it will curve or uncoil itself upward along the spine until it reaches the crown chakra. Once there, the chi energy or kundalini energy then overloads the brain with its energy causing a spiritual experience to occur.

The human energy field or the aura takes on and creates geometric shapes around our physical bodies when our energies are aligned and create what is known as the **Merkabah**. The word **Merkabah** or sometimes spelled *Merkaba* or *Merkava* is from both Egyptian and Hebrew origins. To put it more simply, 'Mer' means a light that rotates within itself, 'Ka' means spirit, and 'Ba' means the body. In other words the Merkabah is the light vehicle that transports the light body or spirit body to higher planes of existence without the physical body ever having to move. Your true essence locked within your physical body is made of light, you *are*, and *have* a spirit body, sometimes referred to as the astral body. [See figure 3.21.1] The Merkabah, to be more precise derived originally from Hebrew words meaning "chariot" or "throne," is a mystical and spiritual concept within Jewish mysticism, particularly in the Kabbalistic tradition. It refers to a divine chariot or vehicle described in Ezekiel's vision within the Hebrew Bible. The Merkabah is often times associated with ascension, divine connection, and the journey of the soul toward higher spiritual realms in Kabbalistic meditation practices.

[Figure 3.20.9]

The concept of the Merkaba has its origins in the Biblical Book of Ezekiel, where the prophet Ezekiel describes a powerful vision of a divine chariot. In **Ezekiel 1: 4-28**, the chariot is carried by four living creatures (often understood as angelic beings or cherubim), each creature with four faces (**a man**, **a lion**, **an ox**, and **an eagle**) and accompanied by spinning, glowing wheels that can move in any direction that's full of eyes. The description of this vision became the foundation of Merkabah mysticism, an esoteric form of Judaism that flourished between the 1st and 10th centuries CE..

[Figure 3.21]

In the later Kabbalistic teachings, especially those influenced by medieval mysticism, the Merkaba is sometimes seen as a vehicle of light that can be activated through spiritual practices, thus allowing the soul to journey through the Sefirot (the ten emanations of God's divine attributes). This concept is akin to the modern spiritual idea of the Merkaba or sometimes called the Merkavah, represents the balance of both male and female energies, as well as the unity of spirit and matter. The Merkaba encapsulates the energy fields of the human body. In the New Age movement, the Merkaba has gained great significant prominence as a meditation tool for spiritual awakening. One of the most prominent figures who revived the Merkaba in modern times is Drunvalo Melchizedek.

[Figure 3.21.1]

This Kundalini Awakening is Sanskrit for **"she who is coiled"** or **"coiled snake."** During deep meditation, the spinal fluid becomes electrically charged and awakens the Chi energy which then begins to move up the spine in an uncoiling like motion. This mystical awakening process is known to be associated with a serpent for thousands of years because of what the serpent has represented since ancient times. The serpent has long been associated with rebirth and transformation because it sheds its skin and becomes a new being. The very same thing happens exactly during a Kundalini Awakening. Once you reach a higher state of enlightenment you are not the same person. You are now connected to the infinite and eternal and realize that all things come from one source and you are then connected to everything in the universe including that one source. When you awaken to who and what you truly are and re-discover your true purpose you then become that new being. Dr. Dispenza teaches this amazing meditation in his book "Becoming Supernatural" and I highly recommend it to anyone on a spiritual journey.

Chapter 4: Aetheric Energy And The Power of Intersecting Lines

Aetheric Energy

Because of the research of open minded scientists like Dan A. Davidson, we now know that shapes, whether to be physical or non-physical, can convert aetheric energy into nuclear forces such as gravity, magnetism, and electricity. Davidson discovered that when two or more lines intersect or converge, there is an increase in the magnitude and concentration of aetheric energy flowing through those intersecting lines. Before we go further, I want to make sure you understand what aether is because understanding aetheric energy will make the rest of the information make sense as you read further in this chapter. Aether or sometimes spelled Ether is a form of energy you will never hear being talked about or taught in school. Aether is energy, a wave that fills and penetrates all space and is the medium for which all the other natural forces manifest and work through, such as gravity, electromagnetism, weak nuclear forces, and the strong nuclear forces. In **1687**, **Sir Isaac Newton** published his infamous scientific findings on gravity which he called **Principia**. In the publication, Isaac Newton stated that Aether was the medium for how gravity worked. In **1704**, he published **Opticks**, which was his study on light. He mentioned that Aether was the medium that light itself used to work through. Every scientist around at the time was very much invested to find concrete evidence of this mysterious energy. The concept of aether was prevalent in scientific thought up until the late 19th and early 20th centuries. However, with the long anticipated advent of Albert

Einstein's famous theory of relativity and advancements in physics, the need for aether as a medium for light propagation was very largely discarded. The concept of "aetheric" or "etheric" energy has its historical roots in ancient philosophy and science. In the past, ancient philosophers and scientists proposed the idea of there being a medium that fills space and allows the transmission of light and several other electromagnetic waves. This hypothetical medium was called "aether" or "ether."

[Figure 4.0]

A few centuries later, in **1887** two scientists we all talked about in our schools, A. Michelson and E. Morley conducted experiments to detect aetheric winds using a interferometer and the experiment failed badly, which later became known as the Michelson-Morley Experiment. By the time the 1900's came around physicists had no choice but to conclude that Aether doesn't exist and very soon after created particle physics theories without including Aether. What led to the study into the Aether in the first place was the question; if there is empty space in the universe, and light is known to have wave properties, then what is it exactly that is waving or causing the wave to occur? There are three measurable properties of wave motion and they are **Amplitude**, **Wavelength**, and **Frequency**. We're not going to get way too deep into each property just thought you should know that. Let's use light for example.

Light is made from very tiny particles called photons. Photons have different wavelengths because there are different colors of light, and every color has a different frequency, which means it has a different wavelength. To put this more simply, every known wave has a medium through which it travels. For example, sound waves travel through the air, so sound waves are the motion of moving air molecules. Water waves or ripples travel through the water and are the motion of moving water molecules. During an earthquake, seismic waves travel through the earth. So, in essence, if every other wave has a medium through which it works, does Aether or ether truly exist?

The reason the famous Michelson-Morley experiment had failed is simply because the two men didn't include what is known in physics as **length contraction**. To put it more simply, suppose that there are two observers and they are moving relative to each other. The observers themselves don't agree on how much time has passed between events or how much space is between those events or things, but they still measure things correctly, yet neither of them is wrong. The overall length of an object moving in or at relativistic speeds undergoes contraction along the dimension of its motion. This simply means that an observer at rest [that is relative to the moving object] would observe the moving object to be a lot shorter in length. Even clocks moving relative to an observer can appear to run more slowly compared to the clocks that are at rest and relative to the observer. This is what we know in physics called **Time Dilation**. Everything is relative.

Aetheric energy consistently permeates through all space and time, acting as the spiritual glue and spiritual substance, forever shaping and binding all multi-dimensions and the laws of those individual multi-dimensions together. Some of us with spiritual understanding comprehend that Aether/Ether exists as an emanation of the mind. Not the brain, but the mind. During the medieval period, Aether was known as the ***quinta essentia***, which is translated to mean **'fifth element**.' It was believed that the earth was made from the four elements: earth, fire, air, and water, with Aether being the fifth element. Think of Aether like this:"

Example: There are infinite versions of you but just for a moment just Imagine there are only two versions of you. The first version is of course you that's reading this, operating in this three dimensional world so therefore operates within three dimensional laws. Now, imagine the second version of you is living in the fourth dimension and therefore operates in fourth dimensional laws. Neither version of the two selves will ever know the existence of the other. Aetheric energy acts as a threshold keeping balance and divine order between both physical and spiritual laws and worlds making sure nature and all of creation obeys those laws not falling under or over God's default threshold.

Aether can manifest in a myriad of ways. As powerful as this energy is, even our thoughts can influence the manner in which this force behaves. I think it is important for you to know that certain materials block our aura and aetheric energy. There are natural clothing materials such as cotton, silk, wool, and leather that all conduct our aura and aetheric energies. Fabrics such as polyester, plastic and acrylics block aura and aetheric flows. For some reason the human aura cannot penetrate through plastic material. The universe only exists because consciousness exists, and without consciousness, the universe simply cannot exist. This amazing knowledge of manipulating this energy was known to the ancients and has since been forgotten, and we're trying to rediscover it today. Shortly after the failed Michelson-Morley experiment, the proof of Aetheric energy had been established, as well as several inventions created to test its existence during the start of the nineteenth century. Credit goes to John Keely, Wilhelm Reich, and Viktor Schamberger for these developments. During those days, the name for Aetheric energy wasn't called Aether but Orgone Energy. Ironically, the studies in quantum physics made a huge leap in studying Aether and have finally proven its existence in modern-day science.

However, it no longer goes by the infamous name of Aether nor orgone energy. Today you may know it by its new name: **Zero Point Energy**. Scientists changed the name to zero-point energy from orgone energy because they didn't want to admit they were wrong. Now, you are about to learn how simply the drawing of lines can influence this energy

The Power Of Intersecting Lines

Scientist Dan Davidson did an ingenious experiment by taking nine chopsticks and sticking them two inches into a Styrofoam ball. Davidson used an Alpha laboratory model three tri-field meter and the measurements were:

- Electrostatic field
- each chopstick had 40 volts/meter
- All 9 chopsticks into ball generated 250 v/m
- 1inch from ball has 1 milligauss or 0.01 microteslas

9 Wooden Chopsticks Stuck into styrofoam ball

Styrofoam ball 2 inch diameter

MEASUREMENTS
Electrostatic field
Individual chopstick has 40 volts/meter
9 chopsticks into ball generated 250 v/m
Magnetic field
1 inch from ball has 1 milligauss or 0.01 microteslas

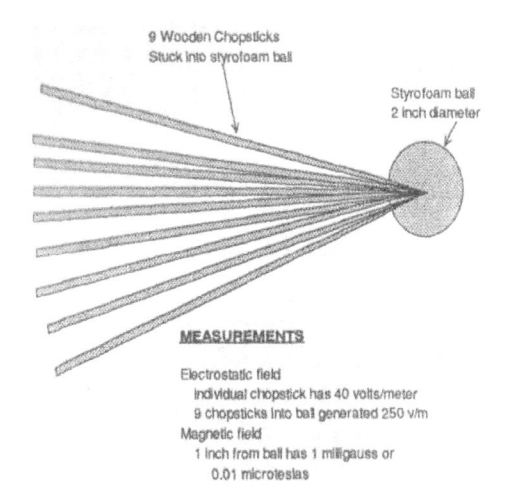

Image from Dan Davidson's "Shape Power"   Figure 4.1

A second experiment was also done to prove that the hypothesis of multiple drawn intersecting lines will generate both magnetic and electrostatic fields. Two types of pyramids were created. They were a paper pyramid and a fiberglass pyramid with 4-inch bases that had other proportions equal to The Great Pyramids. Each side had lines that went from one side of the pyramid and converged in the lower corner of the base of the pyramid. [As seen in figure 4.2 and 4.3]

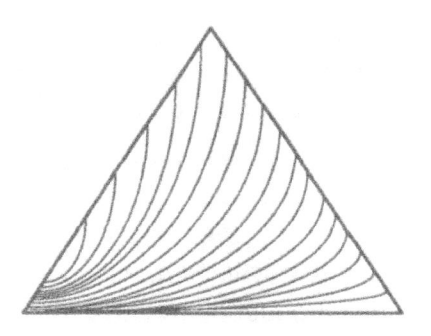

Image from Dan Davidson's "Shape Power"   Figure 4.2

	Fiberglass pyramid with lines	Stack of 19 paper pyramids with lines	Single paper pyramid
Gamma	310	323	0

Image from Dan Davidson's "Shape Power"   Figure 4.3

Just to give you all a more clearer idea of Gammas; according to magnetic anomalies, the size or magnitude of the Earth's magnetic field varies dramatically with latitude, from 25,000 gammas at the equator all the way to 70,000 gammas at the magnetic poles. So the fact that drawn lines on to a piece of paper or chopsticks and Styrofoam can generate gammas is completely astonishing and jaw dropping. Both electrostatic and magnetic fields shouldn't even be present let alone even possible by simply drawing lines on a single sheet of paper, but it's clear that manipulating an unseen, untapped energy is very possible.

Harnessing the hidden powers of lines, geometric shapes, mantras, amulets, talismans, sigils, or (signatures) of elemental spirits and celestial beings has been a very closely guarded secret for those practicing ceremonial magic, shamans, and tribal chiefs since the dawn of creation. The ancient ones who possess this old esoteric knowledge carefully pass it down to select chosen individuals. Mantras especially, they are very closely guarded because there are a few who understand there is a natural power in the form of words and sounds. Mantras are words or sounds produced to influence some kind of mystical or divine event, which brings me to **words of power**. By knowing and understanding words of power, by speaking, singing, or chanting specific words or sounds in a very specific sequence, intonation, even pronunciation, it can cause supernatural phenomena to occur. See, words are two-dimensional but can then raise their frequency to three-dimensional to affect matter. In ancient Egypt, the ancients believed that the god Thoth was the keeper of these words of power. For example, when Isis's child was fatally stung by a scorpion, she spoke specific words and then caused the poison to be expelled out from the child's body. In Christianity, when we read **'The Book of Enoch**,' we see how it explains some of the angels lusted over human women, had sex with them, and in return, they taught them spell-casting, magic, and other secrets of heaven. There is one experiment where we see exactly how two-dimensional thoughts or words manifest into three-dimensional reality and have an effect and influence on matter, and that is the **Rice and Water Experiment**

Instructions:

1. Fill two jars halfway with [cooked] rice. Add enough water so that the water covers the rice, then Screw on the lid and place them in an area in your house sitting next to each other but out of your way.

2. Label each of the jars. Write "love" on one, "hate" on another, or label one jar "good" and the other jar "bad."

3. Every day for one month, spend time speaking to each jar of rice individually. To the loved one, say only good things, To the hate one, say only cruel things.

As the days go by, within that thirty day period you will see the jar you speak good things to, the rice will sprout and flourish, while the jar you speak bad things to, the rice will rot. This is a great visual aid to see just how our two dimensional thoughts can raise their vibrations into a three dimensional space. This experiment is also very helpful when teaching children just how our words can affect people and the things around us. Having children understand this concept at an early age, it will always be a part of them all the way into adulthood. To take it a step further and what is even more interesting in itself is that if you wanted to do this experiment with three jars of rice but with the third jar being ignored, something interesting happens. You will speak badly to the hate jar and speak only good to the love jar, but if you ignore the third jar and not say anything to it at all, it will be even more rotten than the hate jar.

Now let's dive back into the power of intersecting lines. The reason behind this mystical phenomenon is understanding the natural flow of how energy itself flows throughout nature. The flow of Energy flows in a toroidal or spiraling motion. In ceremonial magic if you ever notice in a movie or television series every symbol or drawing is geometrical and symmetrical. Tell me, have you ever seen a ugly random drawing of a magic symbol or sigil? There is a reason for that. It is a hidden reason why every magic symbol or sigil that you see whether in the media or in books, look like they have been drawn by a geometry teacher. As we just learned, when lines are drawn in specific ways or patterns, small magnetic and electrostatic fields are generated, and if these fields are being generated, then no matter how small or weak they are, energy is present.

The Rule Of 4

Herbert Weaver wrote in his book "***Divining, The Primary Sense***" he recalls an account where a dowser by the name of Lawrence Veale simply drew four lines and those four lines will block the signal or the energy from a "witness" to the person it was attuned to. In ceremonial magic the terminology witness describes and refers to any object that is from a specific person and handled by that specific person and *only* by that specific person. Examples of this are: **hair, comb, fingernail, saliva, tooth etc**. Davidson had conducted an experiment on the rule of four using clairvoyants and clairsentients. Then, Davidson instructed the psychics to use their abilities to both see and feel the energy around a glob of his saliva placed on a piece of paper. As he got closer the energy signature got stronger and as he got further away the signature became more weaker. The psychics can see and feel the energy connection between the saliva and Davidson. Davidson then drew four lines around the glob of saliva and the energy blanked out but was still present. His extensive research had also revealed that in order to completely block that connection, at least four drawn squares, dots, or simply symbols on a sheet of paper had to circumscribe the object or witness. If I were to draw a circle on a sheet of paper or any kind of surface and specifically start from the bottom and then begin to draw it clockwise, energy will accumulate and gather or be concentrated in the center of that circle. Now if I take that same circle and draw a triangle or let's say the star of David in the center of that circle for example, [Figure 4.4] the energy will be even stronger this time being focused directly in the center of the triangle. If you look in the center of the triangle you will see that the shape is a pentagon. It is a shape within a shape, within another shape. This shows that we can definitely use symbols and shapes ultimately to interactively intensify an aetheric energy and then convert it into any force we want since all forces are modes from aetheric energy. Intersecting lines and certain shapes create a steady increase in the magnitude of the aether, and hence a magnetic field is created. Understanding this, as well as energy flowing in curved motions or in spiral vortex-like patterns, and the manipulation of those spiral patterns, can possibly lead to a worldwide breakthrough in studying demystifying crystal energy, ancient pyramid energy, unlocking those hidden esoteric secrets of ceremonial magic, and tapping into an unlimited supply or energy source that can potentially power our entire planet, or maybe something that is even more abundantly greater, like a breakthrough in our basic and very primal and limited understanding of space-time and time-space. Just thinking about the infinite possibilities is indeed endless.

But if I'm being completely honest, humans aren't ready for such power and breakthrough in the manipulation of cosmic forces in that area of scientific advancement. Humans are probably thousands of years away from even beginning to understand the basics of this kind of cosmic manipulation. Davidson explains in greater detail his experiments on shapes and intersecting lines in his treatise "Shape Power." Davidson's research has blown the door wide open into the spiritual by demonstrating how this unseen energy works.

[Figure 4.4]

Chapter 5: Entering Other Dimensions; Space-Time vs. Time-Space

Dimensions

Dimensional levels are separated by ninety degrees. In order for one to ascend or descend in dimensional levels, there has to be at least a 90-degree shift in consciousness or two forty-five degree turns/shifts (45+45=90). The Chakras themselves are separated by ninety degrees; musical notes are separated by ninety degrees and so on. To be clear, when I say *dimensions,* I'm not speaking about or really referring to the mathematical understanding of the x, y, or z, axis concept; or easier understood as being length, width, or depth per se, but in a much more broader sense of our relative perceptions of where we are exactly in reality, or realities, and those operations or functions within both time and space. I will soon break down the difference between space-time and time-space shortly but first it will be easier to give a few basic examples of what I mean when referring to dimensions.

Example1: When you use a radio, you turn the dial on a radio to go from station to station. You can then look at those individual stations as different dimensions or realities, and with each turn of the dial you are therefore tuning into those different dimensions or realities.

Example2: There are exactly 88 keys on a piano. Imagine each key is a different dimension, a different reality, a completely different world. We know that one note to the other is ninety degrees. Let's say that middle C is the world or the dimension that we are currently living in, and that dimension is vibrating at 261 hertz. I then decide that I want to visit the next world [piano key] on the scale which is D, and the frequency of that world vibrates at 293 hertz. In order for me to attune from one dimension to the other, or transition from a C note to a D note, I have to make at least a 90-degree shift in consciousness to cross the threshold to step over into that plane, which is D, which is 293 hertz.

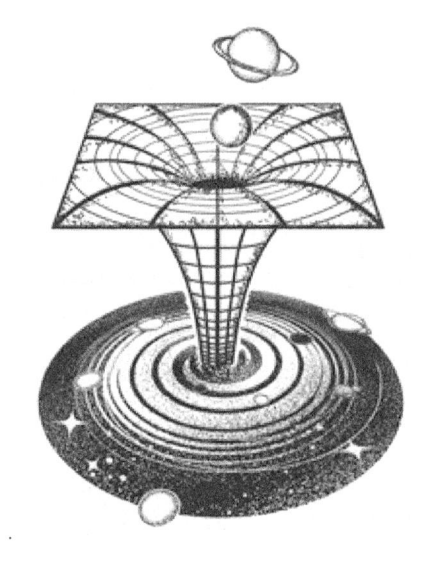

[Figure 5.1]

Space-Time vs. Time-Space

Within this three-dimensional universe that you currently live in you experience the people, places and objects in your environment because you rely on your five senses to make sense of it. Even time itself. Your five senses shape how you perceive your reality and the patterns within your reality. In other words, your physical senses is what allow you to even experience physical reality. The moment you take all five senses away then you cannot experience reality. What if I asked you how do you experience time? When we begin our day every single day, how do we all as human beings experience time? Our scientist tells us, whether it's deep into the vacuum of space or inside the nucleus of a cell, the universe is mostly filled with empty space, infinite space that is always and forever expanding. But what if I told you that empty space isn't truly empty at all but contains a bunch of information within it? This was discovered while studying the electron which I will go into shortly. Time is related to space and space is related to time as you will soon see, but how we experience time is by moving through space. If you are reading this book in your car, in your room on the bed, or simply anywhere, you are in space. You are an object that takes up a position in space no matter where you are even if you are outdoors. You will always be an object that takes up a position in space, which now brings us to space-time.

Space-time can be looked at like this, imagine that you are home on the sofa watching your favorite show. You suddenly become thirsty and decide to go into the kitchen and get something to drink. Earlier I asked how you experience time; well, this is how. You experience time by moving through space. To put it simply, If the sofa is point A and the kitchen is point B, in order for you to *experience* how long or short time is you have to move through space or move between two points which takes time, where you currently are and where you will end up. The faster you move between two points the shorter the time experienced and the slower you move between those two points then the longer the time you experienced. There is actually another way you can experience time. Let's say you don't move at all; you can still experience time by not moving. We all have those days where we just simply don't feel like moving or going anywhere. It is in those very moments you experience time. Why? Because I had just created two points of consciousness in my mind; point A and point B, I'm thinking about where I have to go in relation to where I am. To go just a little bit deeper, I don't truly create two points of consciousness, not really, I only become *aware* of two points of consciousness. That is how space-time is perceived to operate in this three-dimensional reality that we all live in. By moving through space, you experience time and any future moment that is separate from the present moment allows you to become aware of time.

Space-time is also comprised of three variables which plays a part in how we perceive this three-dimensional reality or world that we live in. they are **separation**, **duality**, and **polarity**. People use the words duality and polarity to mean the same thing but of course we will discuss the difference between the two to give you a more concise understanding. **Separation** is how we perceive physical reality as a whole. Everything is just simply flat out separate from each other, using *time* as an example. Time has a Past, present, and future but still are all perceived as being separate moments in time. **Duality** is of the mind. It is the perception of having two opposing things and we perceive those two opposing things to be in constant conflict with each other. For example, there is good and so therefore it must be evil, and they are perceived to be in constant conflict. There is light and there is darkness, and we perceive these two things to be two opposing things that cannot share the same space at the same time. Our eyes only see limited light which helps us to see and try to understand the world around us. We can only perceive the visible light which is a very, very small portion on the spectrum. With the little light that we see, we take that light which we can't see and call it darkness and evil from our very limited view. Also, in duality we tend to see one thing being better than the other. **Polarity** is seeing the bigger picture, us stepping back and seeing reality, objects, and things for what they truly are. Polarity is when you perceive objects, things and forces to be complementary to each other. Like there is light and dark but together they bring us night and day, a magnet has a positive and also a negative side but together they attract. It is the overall holistic view of looking at creation. We perceive creation in separation so much that looking at it through holistic eyes can seems to be an impossible task. Once we learn to master this skill our lives will become less stressful.

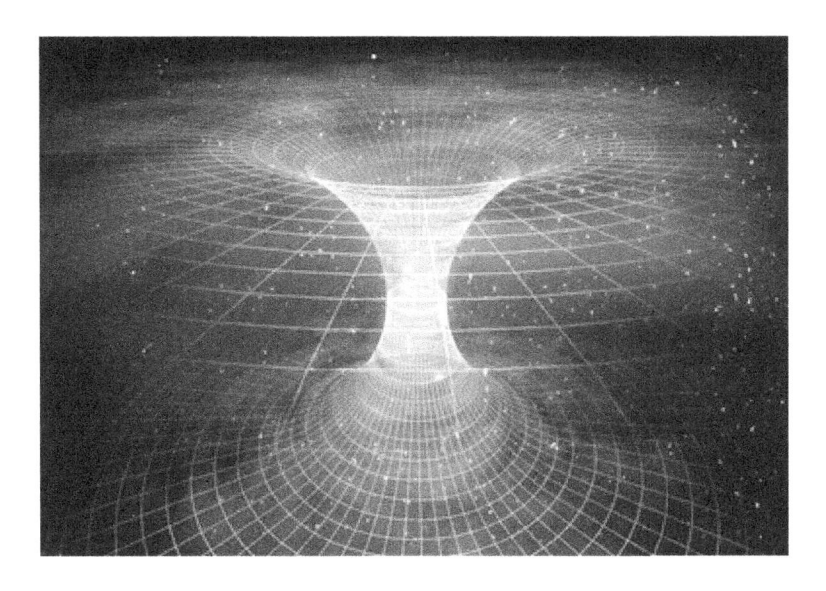

Figure 5.2

Time-space on the other hand operates exactly the opposite from its counterpart space-time. Both science and spirituality agree that in the quantum or spiritual world time operates and behaves much differently. Time is infinite and time is eternal, the complete opposite of how it is perceived within a three-dimensional world. Let's look at this from a more spiritual perspective to make it a little bit easier to understand. We all have had those moments where someone had surgery, and then we hear stories of that person saying that they had witnessed from the ceiling their own bodies being operated on down below on the table. Yet, after these people come out of their surgery, they can't explain to the average individual their experience in detail in a way that makes sense. What if I told you that you wouldn't be able to either? What do I mean? Well, there are those that are advanced in meditation that understand the exact same thing occurs during deep meditation without going under the knife. You See, anytime you have a deep spiritual or a deep mystifying experience, in that very moment you are no longer in a three-dimensional space, so you are not bound by three dimensional laws which means that what you believe to be impossible is now quite naturally possible. The reason why you or nobody else for that matter can explain what you had experience during that spiritual encounter, is simply because that encounter or experience is outside of three-dimensional space and three-dimensional laws. To put it just a little more simply, within this three-dimensional world we all need our five senses to experience this reality. If an individual person has an experience outside of this three-dimensional plane or reality, our five basic senses are not necessarily needed for that particular experience. The more we use our senses the more separation we experience. What does this have to do with time? **Everything!!!**

2 Peter 3:8 NKV

[8] But, beloved, do not forget this one thing, that with the Lord one day is as a thousand years, and a thousand years as one day.

As you can see from the above scripture, *Source*, the creator of our physical three-dimensional reality, functions outside of our three-dimensional reality. Therefore, the true essence of time functions completely differently and outside of all of our three-dimensional perceptions. In other words, from a three-dimensional or physical world sense, time is perceived as linear. Time is linear because there are different ways we can record and measure it in a straight line from a single point, either having a beginning or an end. Once you enter into time-space, time itself becomes non-linear. Through meditation, you will have to become something much more than just a physical vessel or just physical body. You will have to be an experience simply having an experience. When you become just an experience, you will realize that time and all times are happening at the same time in the infinite and eternal now. All those different timelines or events are happening in different spaces or pockets of infinite dimensions. Now, instead of you yourself experiencing time by moving through space like in space-time, you are simultaneously experiencing a multitude of infinite and eternal spaces, which are dimensions, by moving through time. In this reality, separation does not take place; there is absolutely no such thing as separation in the past, present, and future, and the present moment is in the eternal now. In a three-dimensional or space-time reality, time is nothing more than a mere illusion, a spiritual byproduct of spiritual time overflowing into this existence. See, the concept of time constructed by the material brain and how we perceive time is erroneous. How time operates and functions on the spiritual plane is a more precise way to try and understand time. What happens in the spiritual plane manifests into the material plane. These primal creative forces in the spiritual realm are expressed as patterns, and these patterns overflow into the material world. Time is a form of energy, and like many other forms of energy, time moves in a spiraling or vortex-like motion. So, time doesn't exist in the way we think it does, but it exists.

Let's take a moment to think about the old Adam and Eve creation story and see how their fall correlates to time. One day at work as I'm sitting writing this very chapter, I unexpectedly had gotten this epiphany, this sudden rush of knowing or realized perception and understanding surging through me that I am positive could not have been my thoughts. Because it came to me, I knew that in that very moment it was meant for me to share with you. The thought was this: Once Adam and Eve had ate the fruit; their actions would later be called and known for thousands of years to come as "The Great Fall." Now, for a moment think of their lives before eating the fruit. These two were in a perfect state with God himself and they were in paradise, perfect harmony with creation and everything in nature. When you find yourself in the very presence of the Source of all things, The Creator, there is unity; wholeness, balance and most importantly love. You will not experience separation because there is no separation to experience. As soon as they had ate the fruit they fell in consciousness and were no longer vibrating at a higher frequency of perfection, love, and wholeness. When God began to walk through The Garden Of Eden, he then called out and asked Adam where he was. See when God/*Source* called out for Adam,

It wasn't because he didn't know because he is omniscient, and when you are omniscient you have an infinite awareness. But, by asking Adam where he was, it was a method of demonstrating not only this infinite awareness in real time but also outspokenly letting Adam know that he felt a sudden change in his vibration and frequency. Point is, the very moment Source asked Adam where he was it was a clear indication that some kind of change had taken place both spiritually and physically, again indicating that both Adam and Eve fell in consciousness, which is why it is referred to as "The Fall" or The Great Fall. Once Adam and Eve had fallen in consciousness, they were no longer vibrating in a high frequency state with God/*Source*; they were no longer one with *Source*. By dropping in consciousness or a lower state of awareness, their perception will go from having experiences that are *outside* of a three-dimensional reality and space and perceiving life and all of creation much more broadly in its entirety, to dropping down to a three-dimensional consciousness and having a three dimensional perception.

How do we know that? Well, because of separation, duality and polarity. They saw creation in separation. For when you are with *Source*, there is no such separation. Secondly, they now know the difference between being naked and being clothed whereas at first there was no such thing, everything just *was*. They also realized duality; there is good and evil, two opposing things. Since creation, they initially walked with God and had already known what polarity was and *is*, which is everything comes from *Source*, everything is part of a whole but yet not separate from that whole. The overall fall of man was a fall in our overall consciousness as an entire whole. After the fall of Adam and Eve, It had literally meant the way that they had been experiencing simultaneous time, was now being experienced in separate moments after eating the fruit. Just think about how frustrating that must have been for them to essentially go from an understanding that time and all times are happening at the same time(s), to now having to live life and experience life in individual moments.

The Atom In The Quantum

The atom is the smallest unit of matter in the universe. What that simply means is this, if you take matter, and then reduce it to its smallest unit of measurement; it is there where you will find the atom. The atom consists of three very basic subatomic particles known as protons, neutrons, and electrons. The classic model that we all have seen in school of the atom with the electrons rotating or orbiting around the center of the nucleus, similar to how planets orbit around the sun [called the Bohr model] is completely wrong, and the outdated **1913** model is still being taught in school systems today. What we now know currently, is that the atom is surrounded by **99.999999999999** percent empty space. See [Figure 5.3] and [Figure 5.4.] The development of quantum mechanics in the **1920s**, particularly through the hard work of scientists like Louis de Broglie, Werner Heisenberg, and lastly Erwin Schrödinger, led to a more comprehensive understanding of atomic structure. The Schrödinger equation, formulated in **1926**, had provided a quantum mechanical description of electrons in atoms. This led to the development of the quantum mechanical model of the atom, which is now the current and widely accepted model in modern physics.

These discoveries showed that electrons (and all matter) exhibit wave-particle duality, meaning they behave as particles in some contexts and as waves in others, depending on how much they are observed or measured. This duality is a fundamental concept in quantum mechanics and plays a crucial role in understanding the behavior of subatomic particles. Wave-particle duality challenges our classical understanding of reality, as objects in the quantum realm don't really fit into the categories of either "particle" or "wave."

Instead, they can exhibit both characteristics depending on how they are observed or measured.

Bohr vs. Electron Cloud

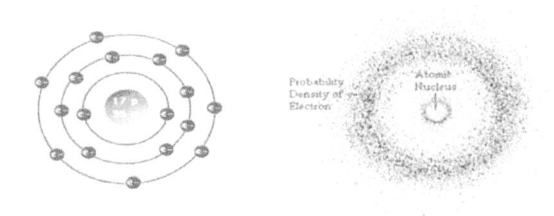

[Figure 5.3]

e electrons
protons
neutrons

electron cloud

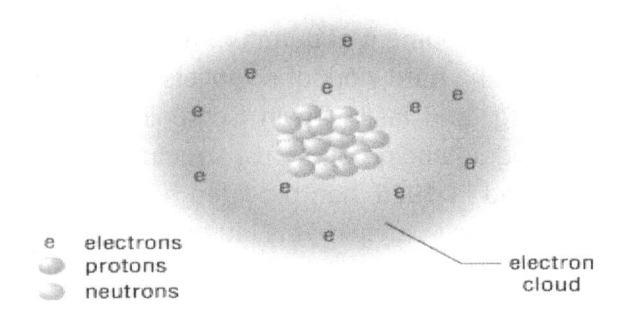

[Figure 5.4]

According to Dr. Joe Dispenza, when describing how small the nucleus or the center of an atom is, imagine the nucleus or the center of an atom is increased to the size of a Volkswagen Beetle; the size of the electron by itself will be equal to the size of a pea. However, all of that empty space itself where that particular electron (could) possibly exist would be the equivalent to 85,000 square miles which is twice the size of Cuba, and Cuba is 42,426 square miles. (Amazing!!).

That is nearly almost impossible to even really comprehend. A few sentences ago I mentioned that all that space is where the electron (could) exist. Let me explain that just a little further. Newfound evidence has shown that the electron first exists as an energetic waveform or simply energy, simply a probability within the electron cloud. This is the mystifying part. To put it more simply, it is only when an observer places their attention on looking for the electron itself is when the electron physically manifests out of the electron cloud. It is only through the very act of observation that the electron materializes into physical matter from an outside dimension of infinite possibility, but when an observer isn't putting their focus on it, it turns back into a waveform and returns to the electron cloud. If you look at figure 5.3, all the black and gray specs are possibilities of where the electron (could) pop into physical reality. Same applies for figure 5.4. It is mind blowing that there is something that can exist as immaterial but yet can localize is beyond words. In science terminology, localize means that something occupies or takes up a position in a given space, and that is exactly what happens with the electron. All physical matter is localized in space. If you are reading this book in your room on your bed, and your physical body is made of matter [like every other person], then you my friend, are a physical object that occupies or takes up a position in space and therefore you are localized. Now, you may ask yourself, is it really impossible to truly predict where the electron will appear next out of the electron cloud? The answer is yes. We can definitely answer that with absolute certainty because of **Heisenberg's Uncertainty Principle,** which states that it is impossible for us to know both the position and the velocity of any particle like the electron because both the position and the velocity cannot be measured at the same time. This breakthrough led to further advancement in the field of quantum mechanics and understanding subatomic particles.

Think of it like this:

Imagine that you are jogging in a park. You bring two friends along, one tracks your velocity, the other tracks your position. It is impossible for the friend tracking your velocity to know your exact position unless you stop moving completely, and it is impossible for the other friend tracking your position to know your velocity unless you are in motion. Everything in this known universe is in a constant state of motion because everything in the universe has a vibration so nothing is truly at rest. So, you see, you can only know one or the other, but you can't know both. Subatomic particles act as both particle and wave. If you throw a rock into a lake, it will ripple causing waves. Waves spread, so therefore you can never say a wave is in just one location, a single point, because it is in motion.

There is nothing that our scientists know of that currently exists that can move faster than the speed of light. Anything that is traveling between two points that is moving slower than the speed of light will take *time*, and therefore, scientists believe that the fourth dimension is time. Time as we know it governs the properties of all known matter at any given point. Knowing any object's position in time is very essential to devising its position in the universe. If an object is traveling at the speed of light, then there can be no such thing as separation between those two given points. Now let's focus on the dimensions that have been proven to exists so far and work our way out from there. We live in a three-dimensional world and there are three-dimensions that have been documented and proven that are within our physical reality that truly helps us to both define and understand the objects and things that are in our overall local environment. Those dimensions are **length**, **width**, and **Depth**.

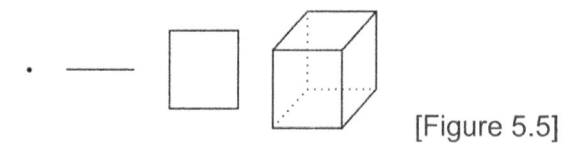

[Figure 5.5]

Understanding Dimensions

If you look at [Figure 5.5] it starts off with just a dot. It has no dimension. Let's think of each shape as its own universe. If I want to get to the first dimension then I would draw a line. This is **length**. If I want to get to the second dimension I would draw a square, and this square *universe* have two dimensions; **length and width.** Now, if I wanted to get to the third dimension, now this *universe* has three-dimensions; **length, width, and depth.** Each time you move into another dimension another direction is added beyond what we can comprehend. You can think of the fourth dimension as being parallel to our dimension. The fourth dimension is an extension of the third-dimension. If you were to look at a square which is two dimensional and were asked to visualize what the square would look like as a three-dimensional object you will visualize a cube. However, if you were to visualize the cube as a fourth-dimensional object you couldn't do it. No one truly knows what it would look like. The brain only understands three-dimensional things so asking it to visualize something outside of its capabilities is inevitable. There are a multitude of infinite universes that are parallel and these infinite universes branch off like the branches on a tree, and those interdimensional branches are interwoven into the very fabric of our three-dimensional reality.

These infinite universes are comprised of the same dimensions as this universe such as length, width and depth as well as the universes that contain those dimensions beyond our understanding. It's hard for most of us to understand that time(s) or past, present and future are all moments in time happening at the time, primarily due to not just our limited understanding and lack of knowledge of the spiritual world, but how we use words in the English language and try to apply them to the spiritual world.

By now you understand that in the spiritual realm, all times are existing simultaneously. But for us to say that those moments are **happening**, we are implying that time has a beginning and end point and this can be very difficult to comprehend. Instead, don't think of simultaneous time as happening but think of it as **existing**. If you were to close your eyes and in your mind's eye visualize a circle; and you were to simply place a dot or points anywhere on the circle, any given point placed on the circle can be defined as either being the beginning point or end point. The shape itself is not defined by having an end or a beginning. Therefore, every single point just simultaneously **exists**.

Every single aspect of our daily human lives, everything that we experience that is responsible for creating our personal reality can all be defined as a circle, and we only perceive and understand reality from only the point from which we are on the circle. Your over-soul is the circle itself. Your soul remembers all of your past lives and keeps track of every version of you in every dimension. There is absolutely no disruption, pause or no break in existence; it continues to infinitely expand in all directions. That means that if the over-soul is the sum total of every infinite YOU in every infinite universe or lifetime, then that means our soul *is* our awareness and our awareness *is* our reality. The true self or sometimes called the over-soul, resides on a higher plane of existence, aware of the sum total of our infinite existence. Each and every version of YOU is simply pin points of awareness, fractions of the total experience.

Scientists often describe time as the fourth dimension in the context of space-time. They believe our reality has three spatial dimensions and one temporal dimension that we call "time," a concept rooted in Albert Einstein's theory of relativity. This view arose from the understanding that in order for us to fully describe the position and movement of objects in the universe, it is believed that we need both the spatial dimensions of how we perceive this reality (length, width, and depth) and a temporal dimension that our scientists label as being *time*. However, Einstein's theory is only partially true. Let's take a look at our earliest understanding of time and why we started considering the fourth dimension as being time.

Here's why scientists consider time as the fourth dimension:

1. **Einstein's Theory of Special Relativity**: Published In 1905, Albert Einstein formulated his theory of special relativity, which introduced the idea that space and time are interconnected. He proposed that time is relative and can vary depending on the relative motion of observers. This theory is what led to treating time as a temporal dimension on par with the three spatial dimensions, collectively referred to as space-time.

2. **Einstein's Theory of General Relativity:** Einstein's later theory of general relativity, was published in 1915, further solidified the concept of space-time. It described how the presence of mass and energy curves space-time, it showed gravity affecting the paths that objects follow. In this theory, massive objects create gravitational wells/bends in space-time, which in turn influences the motion of other objects, including how they experience the flow of time.

3. **Mathematics of Four-Dimensional Space-time:** The mathematics of general relativity as is, naturally treats time as one of the dimensions, alongside the three spatial dimensions. These four dimensions together form a space-time continuum, where the curvature of space-time due to gravity determines how objects move through it.

4. **The Experiments and Observations:** Numerous experiments and observations, were extensively done such as the bending of light by gravity, time dilation in high-speed motion, and even the global positioning system (GPS), which requires accounting for relativistic effects, have provided practical information that seems to support the four-dimensional nature of space-time.

Understanding Simultaneous Time, The 4th Dimension and Portals

As already stated Einstein's theory is only partially correct; though time plays an integral part in our overall physical experience, time should not be considered a dimension or put simply, just one singular dimension. When was the last time you had built something and you used (*time*) as a dimension or you had randomly pulled out a clock to double check your measurements? Time measures intervals by separating at least two consecutive events. It is used to sequence and compare the duration of events. At least that is how it is perceived and believed to work on this plane. It is a man-made construct; a mirage, temporal illusion. So how can an illusion become a dimension? It can't. We might be the only ones in the universe that found a way to measure something that doesn't exists. So in other words it is not used to measure physical objects or matter which is what this plane mostly consist of. Einstein truly wasn't all the way wrong; He just wasn't all the way right either. He just made observations in relation from where he sat on the circle. We experience time as being linear, a linear progression from the past to the present and into the future from point A, to point B, and all the way to point C and so forth. From our perspective it is that invisible thing that allows events to occur and gives us a sense of this natural order and causality. Just as we can move in three spatial dimensions; from the point from which we sit on the circle, we perceive that we also can move forward in time. Even though it only appears that way. If you live in the United States and you call someone in a country six hours away, how come it doesn't take that other person six hours to pick up the phone? Simple, it is because everything exists in the **NOW**. The physical plane as you know it is simply a reflection or a shadow of that which exists in the spiritual. Everything that *is* moving in the spiritual realm is moving and simply existing in the infinite and eternal *now*. Our Scientists believe that *time* is just one individual dimension by itself and that is far from being accurate. The fourth dimension is the dimension where time, space, consciousness [such as the astral plane] and your thoughts and dreams [such as the mental plane] etc., all exist. This is the realm/dimension where all those things just mentioned but not limited to, all come together and merge. It would be wise if our scientists first accept a much deeper concept like *simultaneous time* and then have the spiritual understanding behind the concept. Shortly ago I had mentioned that time is just a part of the fourth dimension. And now you may be thinking, if time is an illusion how can it be a dimension or even a part of? Let me clarify.

I'm not referring to the illusion or concept that we perceive and call time on the physical plane. I'm referring to **simultaneous time** of course. The primal force that exists that allows past, present and future to exist and function all in the eternal *now*. To keep this from being way too confusing, from here on out I will only speak of simultaneous time unless I mention otherwise. Simultaneous time is the true essence of time in its complete wholeness. On this dense physical plane we only perceive simultaneous time through a very small lens of separation and thus it's extremely difficult for us to comprehend it because we perceive it in separate moments. The other reason our scientists are wrong about the illusion of time being just a single dimension is mainly because simultaneous time stretches across several dimensions. To put this more simply, there are a multitude of dimensions that exists along with simultaneous time and because our scientists lack the basic and fundamental knowledge of these basic spiritual concepts, and refuse to openly acknowledge those concepts, whatever weird or strange thing that occurs that can't quite be explained logically or that conveniently fits within the framework of traditional scientific understanding gets lumped under the label of *"time."*

Now let's talk about portals and their purpose within existence. The first thing that needs to be understood is that portals are a naturally Occurring phenomena in nature. There is nothing supernatural or mystical about them as most may believe. As you may already know, portals are like tunnels. They allow a traveler to traverse over great distances from one point to another. However, what most don't know about portals is that they exist within the same realm or plane of reality. They don't function as a bridge between different planes of existence. In other words, they don't allow you to truly travel between the different dimensions nor the alternate universes. According to Dolores Cannon, when you travel through a portal to reach specific locations within the same plane of reality, the traveler will have to undergo a conversion process to access a different plane. Portals are limited or restricted to that particular/specific plane which they exist in. Therefore, an additional step must be taken to transition into another plane. You may be wondering why I'm using the term "planes" instead of "dimensions." Well simply because in esoteric teachings and spiritual terminology/language, when you are using the term "plane," it generally is referring to a very specific plane, versus dimensions which is used in a much broader sense, and a portal's main function is very specific and restricted to the individual plane which it is manifested on. You also may be wondering about wormholes. Wormholes are similar to portals in the way of thinking of them as tunnels. Where they differ, is in the way in which they are used. Wormholes are specifically used for interstellar or intergalactic travel and not local travel like portals.

There are also "dimensions within dimensions." This simply means that there are sub-levels or sub-realities within these dimensions that differ from one to another. These sub-levels have unique characteristics, properties, or rules that set them apart from other levels within that very same dimension. Though this was a lot of information to absorb and understand, hopefully these concepts were added to your overall spiritual awareness and gave a much deeper and a much clearer insight and understanding as the end result, in hopes that you continue your search for the truth and at every step getting closer and closer to *Source*.

Chapter 6: Karmic Law and the Reincarnation of the Soul

We use the term karma in our day to day lives and tell **others** *what goes around comes around, what we do comes back to us in ways we don't expect, for every action there is an equal and opposite reaction*, or *the love you take is equal to the love you make*.

Just think about how many times have you and I have seen people drive trucks with stickers that read "***karma ran over your dogma***". Just ask yourselves, do you really know or fully understand karmic law and karmic experience? Do you understand the cycle of the soul? Have you ever asked why bad things happen to good people? Karma explains and has the answers to a lot of questions that we have always had. A lot of times the answers are either within our own spiritual faiths' and our level of understanding has not reached that level to receive the deeper hidden esoteric truths because we simply aren't ready and certain truths reveal their meanings at certain times. Other times either our pride or ego gets in the way and prevents us from going outside of our Bible or religious book because of traditions, cultural and religious customs. Now, if you are the type that have been religious instead of spiritual, or following traditions instead of truth, then your mindset of course will tell you that having past lives, as well as future lives is something that is impossible, reincarnation is perceived as impossible, there is only heaven or a hell, there is absolutely nothing in between and nothing else, Karma and reincarnation isn't mentioned in the bible or it's not of God etc. Well, keep an open mind and look at this from a perspective from a non-traditional, non-religious mindset and thinking and allow Source to give revelation. We are about to take a deeper look at just how karma and reincarnation ties into salvation and God's will in a manner in which may possibly be new to some of you. People who tend to agree or mostly go with the majority, by historical standards usually turn out to be wrong. Keep an open mindset and don't believe nor disbelieve, simply have your own experience.

[Figure 6.1]

Old Testament scholar Pastor Bernhard W. Anderson before he transcended in 2007 said

"The problem of life is that Man, with his limited wisdom, cannot discern any overall purpose running consistently through life's experiences, he is overwhelmed with the meaninglessness of human existence as he sees it." He further believes that *"the tragedy of life is heightened by the intense realization that the problem of existence must be answered within the brief span between birth and death."*

So, what is Karma? Karma is a natural law that is in majority of every spiritual practice. It is the law of cause and effect that is based upon the deeds or actions you carry out both on the physical and mental planes and it is also the memory of the individual soul.

Examples:

- "For whatever man sows that shall he also reap." **(Gal. 6:7)**
- "He who leads into captivity shall go into captivity; he who kills with the sword must be killed with the sword." **(Rev. 13:10)**
- Buddha: Effects follow their causes as the wheels of the cart follow the foot of the oxen.

Your actions in this life can affect all your future lives. The intent and actions of an individual person [cause] can influence the future of that individual [effect]. We are going to mess up of course, that is a given. A lot of times when we make mistakes people will condemn you and have you thinking that you will go to hell and boil in oil or walk on burning limestone. The effect from causes gets worked out on the very same reality or plain where that infraction or that deed had occurred. It is never over simply because you made a mistake or did something that you perceive to be regrettable because there is such a thing as forgiveness. However, ignorance has a threshold and when that individual knowingly does wrong then that debt has to be paid. However, there is also good karma that has rewarding consequences as well. Oftentimes we hear the word consequence and assume it means bad but in fact that is how society got all of us thinking. Karma deals with rewards just like it deals with infractions. A lot of times it is not God or Source that is punishing us but the consequences of our own actions. It is us that caused an infraction; so therefore, it is us that deal with the effects. It can be something an individual has done ten years prior but if the individual hasn't corrected that infraction ten years prior then the effect can be activated at any given point in time for that individual soul to learn a specific lesson at a specific time. The individual just doesn't know when. We are literally in a school.

I know what you're thinking. Since we will be held accountable no matter what we do, and everything has a consequence then what if we do nothing at all? What if I ignored people and only focused on me and my well-being? just me and my karma?, This attitude may potentially settle or erase my karmic debt but now however I just settled majority of the previous karma just to deal with this new karma that I just created for myself, Helping people and allowing ourselves to become a channel for Source to work through is the more appropriate way to approach karma. We all are here, all of us, for a very specific purpose and for the growth and development of our souls and so contributing to mankind is the correct solution. The goal for all of us as one mass consciousness is to continuously grow every day until we reach the Christ consciousness level and transcend karma completely. Transcend the law of cause and effect.

In **Luke 8:10** Christ said to Luke **"To you it is given to know the mysteries of the kingdom of God, but to others in parables; that seeing they might not see, and hearing they might not understand."**

There are so many hidden truths that are within the Bible and in creation that we don't even realize how much sacred knowledge we actually overlook on a daily basis. Even sometimes when we see the truth that has been revealed; God reveals it to the few, and those few verbally tell someone else. Sometimes the person that is seeing and hearing don't always understand what they see and hear. In the world of science the natural law of cause and effect are observed and so very hard to disprove otherwise. The same law applies to the metaphysical and the spiritual worlds as well. Karma presents the opportunity for us to understand the consequences of our actions and to simply **show** and **be** *love*. There is no other natural law that does this. By God or *Source* creating a system [karma] and putting this complex system into place for the soul to grow by being taught by the deeds the individual person carries out shows that there is no greater act of love. As seen in the opening statement as well as the examples given from Bible scripture, we can clearly see Jesus certainly taught the lessons of karma even if he didn't call it *karma* by name.

John 9 reads, **as he passed by, he saw a man blind from birth. And his disciples asked him,** *"Master, who sinned, this man or his parents, that he was born blind"*? **Jesus answered,** *"It was not that this man sinned, or his parents, but that the works of God might be displayed in him."*

Note: It is here that we see as Jesus and his disciples were walking past the blind man, the disciples asked [who] the sinners were. The blind man himself or the parents. Because they had seen only the effect, which was blindness, by asking who were the sinners, the blind man or the parents? It is here in this moment that the disciples offer two possible *causes* for his *effect*. The basic reason the disciples asked if the parents had sinned is because they knew in the Old Testament it states the sins of the father should be visited upon the sons of the third and fourth generations. So given Jesus' answers as well as the disciples' clues the only other natural way this man could have sinned was before birth in a previous lifetime.

Secondly when Jesus replied, *"It was not that this man sinned, or his parents, but that the works of God might be displayed in him."* This shows divine order. This man who has not sinned nor his parents; was put on a direct path to be healed by Christ at the perfect time. The disciples had a learning moment at a specific place during a specific time and a channel was open for God to work through that was put in place long before the encounter took place.

You have some people who will say and believe that just because the bible doesn't directly teach reincarnation and karma specifically, then we shouldn't believe it. There are quite a few people out there that truly believe that if it's not in the bible it's not true. Here is what I would say in response to that limited perspective. If you have that same mindset every time you open a connection with God, how can you accept the doctrines of the trinity and the doctrines of original sin when the bible doesn't teach those either?? We need to also be aware of the fact that we don't have all of the original teachings of Jesus, like in Acts where for forty days Jesus taught all the disciples the secrets of heaven. These teachings are lost or appear to be lost. Ask yourself this, if you knew the secrets of heaven will you write it all down for just anybody to come and pick up? I hope not. These are the things that are passed down by word of mouth but only a select few are chosen to hear these secrets. In modern times it is said that you are not a true Christian if you allow yourself to believe in reincarnation. First, the Bible does in fact let us know what a true Jew is [**Romans 2:28-29**] but not what a true Christian is. Secondly it depends on what century exactly the individual is basing their perspective on. If you take any modern-day preacher today and you were to drop them somewhere in the first or second century where the earliest Christians at the time openly believed in reincarnation, they will be completely lost and totally confused. It is not a question of can we prove karma. Karma can be observed in nature [cause and effect] and even in our daily lives. Everything in creation *has* and *follows* a cause and effect. The much better question for us to ask ourselves is can we prove the existence of reincarnation? And that is what we are about to take a look at.

What is Reincarnation?

We understand that karma is the energy you put out in the cosmos is the same energy you get back either equal to or amplified either as a sentence for an infraction [wrongdoing] or as a reward for doing a good deed. So how does reincarnation come into play and what exactly is it? Reincarnation is the rebirth of a soul into a new body. It is literally the rebirth of the human soul; a series of lifetimes for spiritual growth, in scientific terms, if we take a look, we'll see that the **law of conservation of energy** states that energy can neither be created nor destroyed - only converted from one form of energy to another. Just as you learned and as explained in chapter one, the soul itself is nothing but pure energy. The evidence of this is in death, for when we die Christians say we go to either heaven or to hell, while others say we are reincarnated. Then you have the few that say we go nowhere at all and we're stuck in limbo. They don't realize they are making the very same argument which is just because your flesh dies your true essence lives. This can be seen in every faith. Whether you are in heaven or hell you are alive in another form, whether you are stuck in limbo you are alive and exist in another form. Reincarnation ties into salvation and has been part of God's plan for all of humanity since the very beginning. The earliest Christians and spiritual practitioners believed in reincarnation but no longer do today in these modern times. Why? When you study the cycle of the soul, God will reveal where in scripture reincarnation is implied by both Jesus and the disciples themselves.

The ultimate goal of reincarnation is to transcend the cycle of birth and rebirth by achieving a state of spiritual oneness with God. This concept is so hard for the modern church to understand because they are misinformed and don't care about learning the concept.

[Figure 6.2]

In the Gospels, Jesus tells his disciples that John the Baptist is in fact the reincarnated soul of Elijah, a prophet who had lived many decades earlier **(Matt. 11:7-14)** *"While they were going away, Jesus began to speak to the crowd about John [the Baptist]. 'I tell you the truth, among those born of women, no one has arisen greater than John the Baptist, for all the prophets and the law prophesied until John appeared. And if you are willing to accept it, he is Elijah, who is to come."*

Here we see that Jesus quotes directly from **Malachi 3:1**, where the messenger clearly appears to be a prophetic figure that is soon to appear. According to **Malachi 4:5**, but if we continue to read just a little bit further, we see that this messenger foreseen is "the prophet Elijah," whom Jesus himself identifies as being John the Baptist. Note that some translations might say his name is (**Elias**). The name **Elias** is a title given to which has two very distinct meanings. The first is that it means forerunner or a preparer. John the Baptist was also given this unique title. The second title is that of a *restorer*.

In the New Testament, the name Elias in its Greek form is the name for Elijah, which is Hebrew. The angel who predicts John's birth in **Luke 1:17** says that John will go before the Messiah "in the spirit and power of Elijah." This will be most modern preachers' rebuttal, saying that John had the spirit and power of Elijah and not actually reincarnated with the soul of Elijah. If you stop at just the physical interpretation of this scripture then yes, this is only partially true. You can see physically through the behavior and the mannerisms to make sound correlations based solely upon the attributes that, that individual person has the very same spirit or power of another individual. However, this perception is flawed and not completely true because you are only focusing on the physical aspects and making judgments based solely upon what you can only see and reasonably deduce. The eyes only see what the brain tells it to see, or what it wants it to see. The physical interpretation and the literal interpretation is only one layer of understanding, however, it is still not the deepest layer of understanding, the spiritual interpretation is.

Remember how Jesus once asked his disciples *"Who do the crowds say I am?"* **They all replied,** *"some say John the Baptist, others Elijah, and still others, that one of the prophets of long ago has come back to life. "But who do you say I am?"* **Peter said:** *"You are the Christ of God."*

It is in this scripture where we get a very clear glimpse of how in depth the earliest Christians spirituality was. They were not dumb at all. The people at the time thought that both Jesus was Elijah and John was Elijah even though they knew that Elijah was killed several decades before. Remember these are the same ancestors that built some of the greatest architectural designs that our modern technology today could not replicate so there is no way a group of that many people could have all been naïve. Reincarnation was sacred, unspoken understanding at its very core and to the earliest Christians and those on a spiritual journey to become one with Source, it was something that didn't have to ever be taught out directly because it simply was just something that was universally accepted as being thee spiritual truth. Reincarnation is vital for the development of the soul and life is a school where each of our individual experiences will lead to a much higher development. A lot of times we go through trials and tribulations and ask God why us? But we never seem to realize that our souls have to go through the experience. Christians today in modern times all perceive that the Bible is saying that you only get one life and everything you need to learn about the eternal you should get it in one lifetime. That is a doctrine that is just simply not true. It takes more than one lifetime to understand eternal destiny and to get rid of karmic debts. Once your karmic debts are settled there is no need for the individual to reincarnate back into the material world because the soul has reached a spiritual level of development where it doesn't have to and it graduates to a higher plane of existence. Just imagine for a moment there was an exception to the rules where one individual becomes saved or reaches a state of Christ consciousness or a high level of spiritual awareness and that individual gets it all right the first time in just one lifetime, what about the majority of the rest of the planet that doesn't get it right the first time in one lifetime? Can you imagine the afterlife with those kinds of odds? That is where the law of grace comes in and ties directly back to God. Everything about karmic law and reincarnation of the soul may sound far-fetched and even a false doctrine to you until you fully understand the law of grace and just how the *Source* of all things connects karmic law and reincarnation into grace.

The Law Of Grace

The spiritual law of grace is what dissolves karma. It is a higher law that transcends and frees man from the law of cause and effect.

In **John 16:33** Jesus says ***"These things I have spoken to you, that in me you may have peace. In the world you will have tribulation; but be of good cheer, I have overcome the world."***

In this scripture Jesus literally shows that he transcended karmic law. In **1st Corinthians 15** Paul tells us that the last enemy to be defeated is death. What exactly is it about the law of grace that transcends and relinquishes us all not just from the law of cause and effect but from the grips of death itself? Well, attached to grace is mercy and forgiveness. Grace as we know is a gift we do not deserve and mercy is not getting the punishment that we deserve. Forgiveness is the power that derives from both grace and mercy and that requires repentance from the individual entity that makes a choice to turn away from anything that can block or sever its individual connection to the higher planes or Source itself. We as people tend to use grace, mercy, and forgiveness interchangeably to mean the same thing and they all have different meanings. Together this primordial triad of God's expression of eternal love comes together and overrides the law we know of as cause and effect. To be clear, when I say law of grace, I'm including mercy and forgiveness in there as well because they work so tightly together. Think of the law of grace like this.

Example: Take time to think for a moment about the law of gravity and how it affects things and think of the law of aerodynamics. Gravity, as you know, keeps things down while aerodynamics lift things upward. In other words, when an airplane is flying through the air the law of aerodynamics overrides the law of gravity so that the plane can lift or fly even though gravitational law is still present.

The law of grace works in the very same way. Grace overrides cause and effect.

Arthur Schopenhauer, a German philosopher once said that:

"All truth goes through three steps. First, it is ridiculed; Second, it is violently opposed. Finally, it is accepted as self-evident."

As we take a look through the lens of history, we will see that especially here in the west we have this notion that we are the most powerful and we know so much more than anyone else and everyone else on the planet is wrong. When the truth is the east whether its Africa, India, or any other spiritual culture have been blessed with spiritual insight from the very beginning. It is the west that is decades behind on spiritual growth and we're still trying to catch up. So, it is okay if one doesn't believe in certain aspects of the human soul returning to incarnate for a particular purpose. The good thing about truth is, truth will never change, and it will always reveal itself in time and will be accepted as truth. What the majority of people think they know always turns out to be wrong and that is the difference between **truth** and **fact**. Facts change over time while truth does not. Truth is absolute, that one concrete answer that lingers in the air that we all are trying to reach upward and find. It will always be absolute and will never change.

Example: In 1930 it was discovered that there was a planet just beyond Neptune lingering in the darkness of space which would later be called *Pluto*. Now, Neptune was discovered in 1846 so if we do the math that means that it took 84 years just for Pluto to be seen. It really wasn't until 2006 the International Astronomical Union (IAU) downgraded the status of *Pluto* to that of "*dwarf planet.*" So, for now only the rocky worlds of the inner Solar System and the gas giants of the outer system will be designated as *planets*.

So now do you see the difference between *fact* and *truth?* When we believe we have all of the information about something it becomes a fact and we perceive it as truth, but truth was in our face the whole time waiting for us to catch up to it. So why is it that Christians or believers in Christ don't believe in Reincarnation when the earliest Christians did? The answer is not as mysterious as you may think if you know church history.

In 553 A.D. during the Second Council of Constantinople which was the Christian church, had decided that the old teachings of reincarnation had no place being taught in Christian churches. It's also key to point out that reincarnation wasn't officially rejected here at this council, but the council had banned many books of the early church fathers who wrote about reincarnation based on the perception that it contradicted the doctrine of resurrection. Many Christian theologians and infamous philosophers that we all have learned about and know of today, who believed in the idea of reincarnation were taught in Alexandria. Yes, home of the Great Library of Alexandria. This majestic library was also divided into the following subjects: **rhetoric**, **law**, **epic**, **tragedy**, **comedy**, **lyric poetry**, **history**, **medicine**, **mathematics**, **natural science**, and **miscellaneous**. The library is believed to have housed between 200,000 and 700,000 books. For those that know the true history of Alexandria this is where some of the greatest minds on the planet at the time both Romans and Greeks came to obtain esoteric knowledge and to be taught by mystery schools. Alexandria was also the primary headquarters of all the other mystery schools. In other words, a lot of sacred and ancient knowledge was all in one location which is why the library was burned twice throughout history. Since we got a basic understanding of the historical significance of Alexandria let's get back to reincarnation.

All the souls created, pre-existed initially in a perfect state with God before incarnating into the material world. Have you ever just asked yourself where the soul comes from? In many ways the soul is inconceivable but what we do know is that it has always existed even though it was created. That sounds confusing right? Souls existed in God and with God in the spiritual realm first before he expressed them outward and they became what we ultimately have come to know as s*ouls*.

John 14 reads:

"Let not your heart be troubled; you believe in God, believe also in Me. In My Father's house are many mansions; if it were not so, I would have told you. I go to prepare a place for you.

And if I go and prepare a place for you, I will come again and receive you to Myself; that where I am, there you may be also. And where I go you know, and the way you know." Thomas said to Him, "Lord, we do not know where You are going, and how can we know the way?"

Jesus expresses to the disciples that they indeed know where he is going. Jesus hints to them knowing of heaven, which is an eternal place, and that they have been there before and only an eternal being or soul can have an eternal experience. Jesus hints to them not knowing heaven, but they understand what they must do to enter its gates. Why would Jesus tell the disciples that they know where he is going as if they have been there before? We see by Thomas's question that he is extremely confused because he is thinking on a mere physical level. So, what does Jesus mean by they know where he is going as if they have experienced being there before? As stated above, all of our souls had pre-existed before physically incarnating into the material world. Everything comes from source, and everything is connected to source. When you incarnate you will not remember anything you have done or places you have been. Thomas's Soul has already experienced heaven and eternity. All of our souls have. Our origin story starts in eternity. We limit ourselves thinking that we are a physical body that has a soul when we are a soul that has a physical body. We deal with physical things everyday so much that we lose sense of our spiritual being.

The physical body was specifically designed and created as a vehicle for the soul to have a metaphysical experience. When you physically can't remember a past life or who you were spiritually before you incarnated into the material world you don't truly forget. What the conscious self doesn't know the subconscious always knows. Thomas himself did not remember being this spiritual entity that originated in heaven because he was using his physical brain to understand.

The human brain is physical matter and truly it can't remember something that it has not first-hand witnessed itself or experienced for itself. There is truly no pattern for it to recognize and the brain remembers patterns and therefore it is limited. What is spiritually happening is this: Right now, imagine you are a soul without being in your physical vessel. You are a soul, and with being a soul, your make-up, the totality of your state of being is eternal and your consciousness is infinite. Everything that makes up your eternal and infinite state of being can fill up every space and room in a mansion. Now, the physical body that your soul will incarnate in has the space of a two-bedroom apartment. So, everything that makes up your massive spiritual identity cannot all fit inside of this physical body because the physical body is limited and wasn't created to be eternal or hold infinite consciousness, it was only created as a vehicle for the soul to have a metaphysical experience.

All the abundant things that make up your spiritual/astral body have to be suppressed into the subconscious mind causing some of your identity to become lost and what sometimes gets lost more often than not, is our memory upon incarnating here. What the conscious doesn't know the subconscious always knows. The true identity of who you truly are as a primordial spiritual being is buried deep inside of your subconscious. The good thing is, this lost memory is not permanent and there are ways to access it which brings us to past life regression.

Chapter 7: Past Life Regression, Memory, and The Akashic Records

Past life regression is hypnotherapy that takes an individual person back through time to their previous life times or incarnations by accessing those memories and those experiences that are normally hidden deep within their subconscious mind. Just like the brain collects and stores memory the subconscious mind also has a collective of stored hidden memory as explained in the end of the last chapter. Scripture teaches that curses and problems can fall upon and follow future generations. You yourself may be going through something that you may quite not understand and a past life regression can be used as a tool for spiritual growth. During a regression there is no way to tell what you are going to experience because every soul is different and every soul has its very own unique divine path and purpose. Memories are deeply intertwined into emotions. Think of hearing your favorite song or just a song that is somewhat very familiar to you. When you hear that song you are brought back to that moment in the past and it feels like your whole state of being is back in that very same moment as if you truly never left. Everything works together and everything we know is interconnected. The brain records certain details and events into our neurons to help us learn from situations, and then those memories are then recorded and stored as learning experiences. This is why karma can be thought of more from a perspective of memory than just infractions or rewards from our actions alone. Past lives and karma are very closely associated and so very tightly knitted to one another that both work for the development of the soul. Think of past life regression like this:

Example: Think of every grade you have been in from kindergarten to a senior in high school. Each time you move up or go to the next grade, the grade level before can be thought of as a past life experience. Every time you advance to the next level you bring the experiences and the memories from that grade level before. Reincarnation is to karma as karma is to memory. This is the spiritual role that memory plays in the development of the soul. This is how memory works on a much bigger scale. Let's take a look at the following scripture.

John 3:13

And no man hath ascended up to heaven, but he that came down from heaven, even the Son of man which is in heaven.

When we take a look at the previous scripture above we naturally understand what it literally or physically means, but once we begin to open ourselves up we begin to decipher what is the deeper meaning behind the spiritual interpretation. We will see that it is saying that no man has ever *ascended* into heaven that hasn't *descended* from heaven *first*, including Jesus/Yeshua himself. If we break this spiritual meaning down even further we will see this means the reason we descend from a spiritual place first is because life itself starts in the spiritual world with Source, Jesus began his life in the spiritual first. Every soul begins its life in heaven first. Once a soul descends down into the physical world it experiences the physical world until it's time to ascend back into the immaterial world. Just further proof that we already exist as immaterial first. Now let's get back to memory.

René Hen, is a PhD professor of psychiatry and neuroscience at Columbia University Vagelos College of Physicians and Surgeons, and Jessica Jimenez, an MD/PhD student at Columbia decided to do an experiment on why memories are attached to emotions so strongly. Some believe that because the physical brain is finite we should only remember what is important to our future well-being. The professor and student chose to trigger fear for this particular experiment so they began the experiment by placing mice into new, frightening environments and recorded the activity of hippocampal neurons and how they stretch to the brain's fear center known as the amygdala. The hippocampus is a part of the brain found deep inside of the temporal lobe where new memories are constantly encoded and the amygdala helps determine what memories to store and it plays an integral part in then determining where those particular memories are stored based on whether we have a strong or weak emotional response to the encounter. What was found was that the neurons that initially responded to the fearful environment, the mice sent those neurons to the brain's fear center which is the amygdala. What was astonishing is that when both the mice tried to recall the same experience of being in that frightening environment and those neurons activating at the same time, the experiment showed the significance of memory by using fear which in turn revealed synchrony. **Synchrony** is the way in which two or more things happen at the same time. So being in a high emotional environment combined with the triggering of a strong emotional response will activate the neurons the brain already stored from the experience. To put it more simply, the greater the synchrony, the stronger the memory. Though this scientific research is what we have known to be the physical process of the brain processing our emotions and memory, what is happening to memory spiritually? Let's take a journey through the Akashic Records.

Akashic Records

Akashic comes from the old Sanskrit word Akasha which means *aether*. The Akashic Records is a place on a non-physical plane. It is a living field of energy that exists far beyond space and time in the eleventh dimension that contains every potential possibility and probable thought, action, desire, intent, experience and of course memory. Memories that *can* happen, that has already happened, that *is* happening, or things that *will* happen. Literally (Everything) is recorded in the Akashic Records. Before I go any further let me just say that the study and teachings of the Akashic Records is heavily taught in Hinduism and Buddhism and as well as an array of many other religions including Christianity, The Quran and some of the most ancient texts discovered that pre-date religion itself. The truth and existence of The Akashic Records does not belong to any religion or culture. The Akashic Records was created and existed long before the existence or creation of man and before man fell from grace, even before the existence of any religion. The Akashic records or The Book of Life itself in the Christian Bible has been talked about in these following scriptures:

(Psalm 69:28, Philippians 4:3, Revelation 3:5, 13:8, 17:8, 20:12, 20:15 and Revelation 21:27) and in every single scripture has been described as being in a non-physical plane described as a library.

- *Psalm 69:28 Let them be blotted out of the book of the living, and not be written with the righteous.*

- *Philippians 4:3 And I intreat thee also, true yokefellow, help those women which laboured with me in the gospel, with Clement also, and with other my fellow labourers, whose names are in the book of life.*

- *Revelation 3:5 He that overcometh, the same shall be clothed in white raiment; and I will not blot out his name out of the book of life, but I will confess his name before my Father, and before his angels.*

- *Revelation 13:8 And all that dwell upon the earth shall worship him, whose names are not written in the book of life of the Lamb slain from the foundation of the world.*

- *Revelation 17:8 The beast that thou sawest was, and is not; and shall ascend out of the bottomless pit, and go into perdition: and they that dwell on the earth shall wonder, whose names were not written in the book of life from the foundation of the world, when they behold the beast that was, and is not, and yet is.*

- *Revelation 20:21 And I saw the dead, small and great, stand before God; and the books were opened: and another book was opened, which is the book of life: and the dead were judged out of those things which were written in the books, according to their works.*

- *Revelation 20:15 And whosoever was not found written in the book of life was cast into the lake of fire.*

- *Revelation 21:27 And there shall in no wise enter into it anything that defileth, neither whatsoever worketh abomination, or maketh a lie: but they which are written in the Lamb's book of life.*

The Akashic Records, also called "the Book of Life," in the Bible, can be thought of as being a universal or a multi-dimensional "Core" or a "Storehouse" that stretches beyond space and time that stores information from every individual soul across every dimension. It is a dimension of consciousness that only a few chosen have got to experience. Amongst those very few was the late and great Edgar Cayce, the most documented psychic and Christian Mystic in all of history. In order to understand this mysterious non-physical plane of existence we have to dive into the life of one of the most interesting, spiritually anointed men of God to walk the face of the planet and who saved so many people's lives through his work. Throughout his life, Cayce conducted over 14,000 documented readings, where he would prescribe remedies for illnesses, give spiritual guidance, and even predict future events.

Edgar Cayce

Edgar Cayce was a very humble man with an extraordinary gift that every spiritual person who is on their spiritual journey should know or at least heard of. Edgar Cayce was born **March 18, 1877** just south of Hopkinsville, Kentucky. Cayce's gift began at a very early age when he begin seeing and talking to his deceased grandfather on a frequent basis. Cayce's grandmother believed that Cayce had an ability to see beyond the veil and while living in her last days revealed to Cayce that his grandfather had the ability to move objects with his mind without ever touching them. When Cayce was 10 he went to church for the first time and fell in love with everything about God and became fascinated with the source of all things. It was at that very moment Cayce began down a divine path of aligning himself with God. All through his adulthood, Edward Cayce would always have either a newspaper in his hand or a Bible, he taught Sunday school, and once a year for the rest of his life until his death he would read the Bible all the way through. He even prayed that he wanted to help people and be of service to others.

Edgar Cayce

One day while reading his Bible an angel appeared to Cayce and told him that his prayers were answered and asked Cayce what did he want most of all. The frightened young Cayce responded and said he wanted to help people; most of all helping children, and he wanted to become a missionary. The young Cayce continued to display his extraordinary gifts all through his childhood. There was one incident where one of Cayce's teachers complained to his father how poor his efforts were doing in class with spelling and his father knocked him out of the chair. The Angel that appeared to Cayce the night before told him that if he can rest they will help him. Cayce begged his father to take a nap and that's where the young Cayce put his books under his pillow. His father came to wake him up and miraculously Cayce knew all the answers and from that point on he treated all of his school books the very same way. Cayce's father thought he was fooling around and knocked him out of the chair again. By placing books underneath his pillow he was able to recall and absorb whatever was in the book word from word. Shortly after, Cayce was able to diagnose in his sleep. This is where this technique came from.

He was struck on the base of the spine by a ball during a game in school and wasn't acting like himself afterwards. Later that night when put to bed the young Cayce diagnosed himself in his sleep. His parents made the cure and the next day his father bragged to everyone how special his son is. This caused Cayce to be looked at differently amongst his peers. Cayce's parents were uneducated and he himself didn't make it past the eighth grade but he turned out to be one of the most interesting people to ever walk the face of the earth and it all started with just one genuine, selfless prayer to be a service to others. When giving readings Cayce will lie across the couch and go into a deep trance which he will then enter The Akashic Records. This is how he got the nickname "The Sleeping Prophet." In fact, he didn't have to have the client physically in the room with him. As long as he had a letter, item or had something that was personal to the individual he was still able to attune to that individual person and the Akashic Records. As Cayce's spiritual abilities grew exponentially, so did his overall understanding and faith as a Christian. Everything wasn't always easy for Cayce to accept spiritually.

Sometimes his reading will reveal truths about universal laws and the existence of physical creation that he wasn't familiar with growing up in a Christian household. When he would give readings to clients Cayce would lie across the couch, put himself in a trance-like state and enter the Akashic Records. The very first reference in Scripture to this non-physical space is found within **Exodus 32:32**. After the Israelites had committed a grave sin by worshiping the golden calf, Moses pleaded on their behalf, offering to take full responsibility and have his own name stricken "out of thy book which thou hast written." It is later in scripture in the Old Testament we see that nothing about a person that is not known in this same book. In Psalm 139, David makes reference to the fact God has written down everything about him and all the details of his life even that which is imperfect and those deeds especially which have yet to be performed. Cayce will come across things like reincarnation and karma and pause during the trance because they were concepts that were never taught to him or talked about in his church or upbringing. The more and more readings Cayce gave and the more people he helped he realized these principles and concepts are natural universal laws and it all ties back to God the source of all things. These once unknown laws of the universe which at one point were never part of his life, became part of his spiritual growth and actually strengthened his connection with God. Cayce never accepted payment for his readings and for over forty plus years Edgar Cayce had led people closer to Source. His abilities had one condition placed on them similar to the condition with Samson and his hair not being cut. Cayce could not use his powers for personal gain but only use them to help people. He couldn't remember the answers to the questions clients would ask him and there was one incident where a client took advantage of this and caused Cayce to inadvertently use his gifts for personal gain. When this happened Cayce got an extremely unbearable and excruciating pain in his head. From that moment on for every session that was documented Cayce had his assistant and his wife in the room to watch at all times to make sure it would never happen again.

When discussing the Book of Life, Cayce stated that it was *"the record of God, of thee, thy soul within and the knowledge of same"* reading (281-33). In another reading (2533-8), Edgar Cayce was asked to explain in much further detail the difference between the Book of Life and the Akashic Records.

Question: What is meant by The Book of Life?

Answer: *The record that the individual entity itself writes upon the skein of time and space, through patience and is opened when self has attuned to the infinite, and may be read by those attuning to that consciousness.*

Question: The Book of God's Remembrances?

Answer: This is the Book of Life.

Question: The Akashic Records?

Answer: Those made by the individual, as just indicated.

You can't talk about The Akashic Records without talking about the soul. One inquiring mind may ask, what is the purpose of the Akashic Records? It is to keep track of a soul's journey, its sojourn into multiple lifetimes, particularly the ***memories*** of that particular soul to help assist with each soul's personal growth. God knows all, sees all. It is not meant for source to keep up with but the individual entity and/or the celestial forces that are appointed to guide that entity. From scripture we know that the human soul exists so that one day it can become a companion with source. **In Genesis 1:26** we see that we were created in the image and likeness of the creator. This indicates that (Life) itself did not begin with a physical birth. This means that there was an existence in spirit form prior to our physical manifestation and therefore our natural state is spirit. So to sum it up, each individual soul has its own set of records within the Akashic Records or this universal library. The records are like a precise detailed account of the soul's journey through time and space, including past lives, present experiences and future possibilities.

According to author **Kevin J. Todeschi**

God gave to each soul complete freedom of choice and the opportunity to find expression to find themselves. Because souls are created in God's image, it would only be through a process of personal experiences one choice leading to another, and then another, and then another that God's companions could gain their own individuality, truly being a part of Him and yet individuals in their own right. Once they have discovered their individuality they would once again return in consciousness to be His companions and co creators'. The soul gains firsthand knowledge not only about its own identity but also learns how choices lead to certain experiences. In time, soul, experiences and acquired knowledge will lead to wisdom. Inevitably, wisdom will lead to compassion and eventually love will be the end result. At this point, the soul will know its individual identity as well as its true relationship with God. The soul will have come to understand that its primary essence and God's are one and the same, LOVE."

Cayce taught that karma, the law of cause and effect, can be more thought of as being the collective memory of the soul as it gains new experiences with each lifetime that it incarnates. Karma is patterns of memory that an individual imprints or stamps into the skein of time and space and that is what The Akashic Records is storing. Have you ever asked yourself how do the universe or God know that it's you that did something wrong or good when another individual person can do the very same exact thing? What are the identifying markers that mark you as the individual to be written in the book or recorded in The Akashic Records? It is because every single thought that you have ever expressed, every deed, intention, action, emotion, and desire, etc. All of it in its entirety carries its very own unique vibration and each single individual person vibrates at a very specific frequency or vibration. So in other words, every single time you have a thought, intent or carry out an action your individual vibration gets recorded and imprinted into the skein of time and space and thus you are identified as that individual.

Think of it like a book inside the library. Each book has a specific number assigned to it called a (call number). A call number is like an address and usually found on the spine of the book. It tells us where the book is located in the library. It also has other information attached to it like the author and title and it identifies the book. That is what happens when you imprint your energy and vibration into the very fabric of the infinite universe. You are unwittingly releasing identifying markers that are only attached to *you* with every single action, deed, thought, emotion, and intent. The Akashic Records is a dimension of consciousness that contains a vibrational record of everything. If you are still confused about how is it possible for the universe to have or store information, think back to chapter one. All frequency, energy and vibration contain information within it. When you print your vibration in the universe it is the information that is within it that gets processed and is recorded.

Before his untimely death in 1945 Cayce had created a hospital, a university, an oil company, gave close to almost 20,000 readings, cured thousands of patients with illnesses by psychically diagnosing them and had well known celebrity clients such as Marilyn Monroe, Nikola Tesla, Woodrow Wilson, Nelson Rockefeller, John D. Rockefeller Jr., Irving Berlin, the Great Harry Houdini, George Gershwin, and Thomas Edison. Cayce was even rumored to have known the famous authors Mark Twain and Edgar Allen Poe. By

1970 there were at least 12,000 of his predictions that came true and a little over 2,000 predictions that hadn't happened yet. Out of 12,000 readings he only made one tiny error and it was his ONLY mistake. Cayce received a letter from a man in France asking for a health reading, but Cayce mistakenly gave a reading on the client's twin brother. There is a very good reason this happened but that's a story for another time. The Great Nikola Tesla once said:

"My brain is only a receiver, in the Universe there is a core from which we obtain knowledge, strength and inspiration. I have not penetrated into the secrets of this core, but I know that it exists."

Cayce gives us another insight into the function of The Akashic Record which is potential probabilities and possibilities of destined paths based upon the infinite choices of the individual person. For a moment imagine computer software or a program that was created that can truly predict with extreme precision and accuracy of all the potential possible and probable choices that you will make. The program can analyze the consequences of those particular choices and foresee the effects of how those choices affect the people and environment around you. This nonphysical plane of existence was ingeniously created as a way for the soul to go through a process of growth and soul development by ever developing timelines of the potential probabilities and possibilities based upon the choices that are consistently made by the individual person, with The Akashic Records being a dimensional field of consciousness that in many ways is alive. We continuously and casually seem to use the term *consciousness* in our everyday conversations and I think that it's time that we dive a little deeper into this esoteric concept to truly get a more clear, more basic, and more holistic spiritual understanding of what consciousness actually is. Our thoughts; emotions, and our experiences pass through our brain over a million times a day, thousands of times per second, and most of what we experience with the five senses is mostly our physical consciousness. Being an eternal spiritual entity you have a dense physical or material body.

Spiritual consciousness is you becoming aware of your true spiritual self and then recognizing your connection to *Source* and all things in existence. Let me remind you that you are so much more.

Chapter 8:
The Mind vs. The Brain

The brain is a physical organ but the very mind itself is not physical matter. The brain is the physical place where the immaterial mind resides. The physical components that make up the brain either by themselves or as a whole cannot comprised of every single thing that makes up the human experience. The mind and the brain are both separate but inseparable just like it's impossible to separate energy, frequency and vibration. The mind is mostly composed of but not limited to our consciousness, the intellect, six senses, will, thoughts, emotions, and subconscious/soul. All of these things come together to give us that human experience. The brain is the conduit or the medium for which the mind works through. These things stimulate the brain every single day of our natural born lives and it is just another example of how the immaterial influences or affects matter. You can think of it like this:

Example: Think of our physical brain as a television and the picture and sounds coming through the television are components of the mind. The sound and audio or (the mind) comes together and works through the television (the brain) and the entertainment you get from both the sound and picture is the (human experience).

The fundamental energies that started all of creation are inside of us and consciousness is one of them. In order to fully understand the two creation stories in Genesis; [there was life before physical existence] one must first know and fully understand the difference between the mind and the brain first, and it is only then, you will see the pattern of God's divine genius of all creation in Genesis. We know that all things came from and originated in God or Source himself, and the soul itself is the very spiritual essence that makes up humankind. We see that in **Genesis 2 verse 7** that Source breathed life into Adam and Adam became a living soul. We can see that the soul itself was given a life force for humankind to exist and the soul then became our spiritual core or our very essence as the end result. See, a body without a soul is a corpse, and a soul without a body is a ghost. As mentioned above we know the mind and the soul are a part of each other and work together which aids us in having the human experience, and we know this because **Proverbs 2:10** gives us the spiritual ground to prove that the mind is a part of the soul. "Wisdom will enter your heart, and knowledge will be pleasant to your soul."

Proverbs 24 verse 14 *"So shall the knowledge of wisdom be unto thy soul: when thou hast found it, then there shall be a reward, and thy expectation shall not be cut off"*. It is here we see that both knowledge and wisdom are part of the mind because a sense of knowing is a matter of the mind it is therefore connected to the soul. So, since the soul already pre-existed *with* Source and *in* Source, that means that everything in creation comes *from* source and the mind is connected to the soul and the mind pre-existed as well. It just needed a physical body to be placed in to incarnate itself in very much like how evil always existed but just needed a platform or vessel to work through. Now we can say that the mind came before the brain or immaterial was created before physical material. If you are still confused, think of it like this.

Example: Try thinking of both the mind and the brain as being the software and the hardware on your laptop. The mind is the software [immaterial] and the brain is the hardware (physical material). The mind gathers, stores, and manages information and this information is the (software) but it needs the brain, the (hardware) to process this information. If you have just a computer with absolutely no software put on it, then what good is the computer? This is exactly how the mind works through the brain. Everything works together. Everything is interconnected. The brain records certain details and events into our neurons to help learn from situations, and in turn those profound memories are then recorded and stored as learning experiences.

Consciousness

What is the human Consciousness? There are so many different definitions of consciousness. Consciousness is mostly thought of as being aware. Awareness is closely correlated to human perception and the definition of perception means *to become aware of*. So no matter where you look or how you break it down, consciousness is associated with the state of being aware. Psychologists will argue that being aware is a simple matter of our cognition. **Cognition** as we know is the mental process or the ability of obtaining knowledge as well as having the innate ability to comprehend things through our own thoughts and experiences which in turn works through the five senses. There are five basic primary cognitive functions or skills that most of us share and they are as follows: **reading, learning, memory, logical reasoning, and paying attention**. There are many different levels of our awareness or many different levels of consciousness and there are a lot of times, more often than not we tend to only associate our consciousness solely to just our *physical awareness* which can only be experienced, again, by or through the five senses. There are many different levels of awareness or levels of consciousness that go beyond the five senses and beyond the physical world. Physical consciousness is a huge part of the human experience which is made up of the immaterial mind, the soul, and spirit. We shouldn't make the mistake of saying that consciousness is only associated with the waking mental state because you truly don't have to be awake to be aware. If the human body was created in three parts, mind, body, and spirit, then we are then inadvertently associating being *awake,* with just the physical body and choosing to ignore the other two components completely. We also shouldn't associate just one level of our consciousness or our awareness like physical consciousness, to the *entire* makeup of the human psyche or the human experience. Consciousness can simply be thought of as being activity or awareness in motion. Awareness is constantly in motion.

Think of it like this:

When you are getting ready for bed at night you might take a long hot shower, turn your air conditioner on and prepare your body to relax and go to sleep. After about thirty minutes of lying down you drift off, and if you are a deep sleeper you probably might be asleep for a long time. Now several hours go by and at some time during the late-night early morning, your body then begins to get a little cold because you turned the air conditioner on before you went to sleep. At this point you are in a very deep sleep but your body is consciously aware of how cold it is. Your mind's awareness is not focused on the physical world because your mind is temporarily out of commission until you fully awake but your *physical awareness* is there. During your deep slumber you unknowingly reach your arm over and pull the blanket over on top of you to keep warm, all while still remaining in a deep sleep, at no time ever aware of what you just did. This example here is what I mean by there are different levels of consciousness or awareness. This is what I mean when I say you don't have to be awake to be aware. How many times have you gone to sleep and woke up in a different position than when you drifted off? Just because your mental awareness is not always aware of your physical awareness, that doesn't mean that your physical awareness has stopped working completely. Remember, our consciousness or *awareness* is always in motion. Let's think of something a little bit more simple and modern like your cellphone. Chances are you have apps running on your phone. Chances are you also have select apps on your phone that you constantly use like your social media apps. Though you are aware of these apps because you are using them, there are still apps running in the background that you are not aware of. This is a clear and accurate way to look at the conscious and subconscious. The makeup of our spiritual awareness is kind of made up in a very similar manner.

Your subconscious is always in motion working and running in the background, eavesdropping on your consciousness.

Think of consciousness as a sense with senses. It sounds crazy, trust me I know. The old Latin root word for sense is 'sens' which means to feel. Feeling doesn't have to always be associated with a physical sensation or experience. If you were to say that the dog has a keen *sense* of smell of course you're not saying that the dog can literally feel the smell because smell doesn't have a sensation. But understanding that a sense with senses or *consciousness* has faculties I think gives a much broader understanding. When I say consciousness has faculties this is what I mean: When you think of a faculty, think of a school system. The faculty will be the teachers, principal, educators, and professors that are all part of a system that all functions together to help bring us all a material experience. That is exactly what our physical consciousness is. Your physical awareness has five basic faculties: **taste**, **touch**, **see**, **smell**, and **hearing**. These basic five faculties would all work together as a larger system as your physical consciousness so that your physical consciousness or *physical awareness* can perceive a physical experience. Similar to how the school faculty come together to give the student the whole entire school experience. There are different levels of consciousness that help you to navigate through life and each level has and uses different faculties that most of us are still trying to figure out today. From birth, we all have that one layer of consciousness that is responsible for being the moral sense of us, instinctively knowing right from wrong that continuously guides us in our decision making, but it doesn't use the same faculties as the physical consciousness for the experience. This happens on a soul level and not on a physical level. There are levels of awareness and consciousness on the inside of you on a small micro level as well. Humans are created in three parts as we know: *mind*, *body*, and *spirit*. Each of those three primal parts can be better understood by looking at them as being the *conscious*, the *subconscious* and the *super-subconscious* which we will address later, but for now let's focus more on the primary differences between consciousness and awareness. **Awareness** is the state of being cognizant of what is unfolding within your immediate environment and surroundings. It involves recognizing the stimuli in our immediate environment and understanding one's immediate situation. Self-awareness is also a big part of that, you recognizing yourself-actions, your thoughts and your intentions. **Consciousness** comes from a much deeper state of understanding and engagement. It encompasses our awareness, but extends to the ability to also reflect, analyze and then interpret our experiences. It can be easier thought about like this: If you are feeling stressed at work, you become aware of the stress, but it is consciousness that allows you to do more than just recognize it. It allows you to explore, analyze and reflect on how you got to that state of being stressed. So to put it more simply, Consciousness is more holistic, it is the whole, while awareness is a part of the whole.

All your cells operate and function everyday inside of your body. All the different cells in your body have their own individual functions. Nerve cells communicate by sending signals through the body, muscle cells allow you to move, tissue cells defend against bacteria etc. You don't have to instruct your cells to do these things, they just do them. It is because they have their own consciousness, their very own mini brains so to speak, that gives the instructions for you. There are numerous different levels of consciousness or states of mind. When becoming attuned with your awareness/consciousness each individual person is capable of stepping into these different states of mind. I will go further into the different states of mind in a future chapter but for understanding

There is this amazing woman that goes by the name Mary Ann Schinfield, and NASA Scientist are absolutely stunned by her innate abilities. She is legally blind and can still maneuver around objects so seamlessly that no one in the room can tell that she is blind. She also has the ability to allow other people to see through her eyes. Though amazing, that is not the most mind blowing thing about her abilities. Mary Ann has full memory and experiences of her past lives even the past lives in other dimensions and yet that is still not the most mind blowing factor. NASA told Mary Ann the name of a very specific satellite that was in orbit and asked her to tell them the identifying information off that instrument. She then relayed to the scientist the information off of the instrument and was one hundred percent correct. The scientists were stunned because there is no way she could have known the information on the satellite. She is legally blind so she didn't see it on Google or had read it anywhere because that information *was* and *is* not available to the general population publicly. Mary Ann had explained that a part of her consciousness was flying alongside the satellite and that is how she relayed back the information. Her consciousness appears to be on a whole different level, maybe even equal to or greater than that of the great Edgar Cayce. This is an example of different levels of human awareness. This is completely different from picking up a vibe and telling if someone is having a bad day. Our top scientists don't fully understand the intricacies of human consciousness. Well in fact, there are some people that still question the existence of higher planes of consciousness overall even when the evidence is clear. Higher planes of consciousness refer to the various states of awareness and perception that transcends past the ordinary human experience. These higher planes of human consciousness are often described in various spiritual and philosophical traditions and are mostly associated with a greater awareness, deeper insight, and the overall sense of interconnectedness with the universe. While these concepts are widely discussed in the context of spirituality and mysticism, they still are not universally accepted. Mary Ann Schinfield had that very unique ability to be aware of and recognize her immediate environment, as well as the consciousness to also be outside of it as well. Schinfield's experiences also involve not just dimensions of consciousness but interdimensional communication, where she interacted with beings from other dimensions. In one account, she helped NASA track the fragments of the Shoemaker-Levy 9 comet before they collided with Jupiter in 1994

Here are some common ideas and descriptions associated with higher planes of consciousness:

Expanded Awareness: On the higher planes of consciousness, individuals often report a heightened sense of awareness, both of themselves and their surroundings. They may feel more in tune with their emotions, thoughts, and the energy of the world around them.

Unity and Oneness: Many descriptions of higher consciousness involve a feeling of oneness or unity with all living beings and the universe. This can lead to a profound sense of interconnectedness and a reduced emphasis on the ego or individual self.

Transcendence Of Time and Space: There are some individuals that report experiencing time and space much differently than how we experience it when they are moving on higher planes. They may feel as if they are no longer bound by the constraints of time and space and can access information or insights from past, present, or future.

Deep Insights and Wisdom: Higher states of consciousness are more often associated with profound insights, wisdom, and clarity of thought. People may experience a deep understanding of complex concepts and a sense of purpose or meaning in their lives.

Altered States of Consciousness: These higher planes of existence are more often than not reached through altered states of consciousness, which can be greatly induced through meditation, mindfulness, deep contemplation, psychedelic substances, or other known and unknown spiritual practices and rituals. These states of consciousness are typically different from our everyday waking consciousness.

Spiritual Experiences: Higher consciousness is often described in a spiritual context, with many people often report encounters with spiritual entities, divine beings, or a sense of being in the presence of a higher power or intelligence.

Levels and Realms: Some belief systems posit that there are multiple levels or realms of higher consciousness, each with its very own unique characteristics and experiences.

Chapter 9:
Destiny Vs. Fate

Destiny and fate are two of the many words in the English language that we use interchangeably to mean the same thing when we are speaking. Understanding the difference between the two will unveil a revelation about life and creation that you might have not yet thought about. The Bible as well as several other spiritual teachings tells us that there is power in the human tongue and we can speak things into this physical existence. So, if you can speak things into a three- dimensional reality or space for it to manifest then that would have to mean that *everything* in the universe is not set in stone and that there are indeed exceptions. If Source showed that much grace to allow us to have that much power inside of us then there is no limit to what we can do and the only limits we have are the limits we place on ourselves. Spiritually what is the true meaning of destiny and fate? **Destiny** is a multitude of infinite potential possibilities and probabilities of specific events that *can* or *may* occur. **Fate** comes from the Latin word **Fatum** which means **that which has been spoken**. Fate is final, it is what is beyond human control and no human can influence its divine outcome, it's final. Destiny works quite the opposite. Destiny is within human control.

Your life choices determine what path you walk. Throughout life your choices will constantly change causing you to jump back and forth from path to path and you will not even realize what you will encounter on any one of those paths because the lessons to be learned on those paths are unknown until you make the choices that will lead to those lessons. Sometimes we never know the full outcome of our choices or our actions until we are met with the outcome face to face. Let's take a step back and analyze destiny a little more. We know that destined paths are a multitude of infinite potential possibilities and probabilities but what does that actually mean? To put it more simply, imagine in front of you, was an infinite multitude of paths that you *can* choose to take your family to the beach, the infinite choices that **can** be chosen of which path to take are endless.

Now, here is where potential, possibility, and probability come into play. Out of the endless paths to choose from you know you will end up at the beach, so by you choosing in the first place, make it a **potential,** meaning you are *likely* to take one of the paths out of the infinite multitude. Each path is a **possibility** because a choice *could* be made because you have that free choice to choose any path, and each path is a potential **probability** because the *chances* of you choosing that path are based upon a choice or a series of choices that must be made. Two other words that we all tend to hopelessly use interchangeably often are *spirit* and *soul.* We have to unlearn everything we think we know about the universe and life and come back to the drawing board and apply a new approach and a more new age way of thinking that can be applied physically, mentally, and spiritually. When you unlearn it does not mean that you are forgetting, but choosing to crucify the ego to make space for higher thinking and skills to develop. Fate is the end result. It is that of which no human has control. It is completely and utterly unavoidable and there is no choice that can be exercised that can change or prevent it from taking place. A higher power dictates how and when it will all end for each and every one of us. The only thing that we are ultimately responsible for in this life is the choices that we make daily; not how it ends, that is above our pay grade. Think of destiny and fate like this:

Example: If you look at a fork in your kitchen, you will notice that it has four prongs or (points) for which to eat with. Imagine each of those points are *destiny,* each representing a potential probable and possible destined path that you may be on. Now imagine at the tip of the handle is *fate*. It doesn't matter which way you turn the fork, all four points lead to the same handle.

It is so very important for us as spiritual entities that have physical bodies to unlearn what we think we know about ourselves and the life around us, especially when we have a track record of being wrong. If you are born in the United States and you have been taught how to drive on the right side of the road; you might visit The United Kingdom where they drive on the left side of the road. Now, you have to be taught how to drive on the left side of the road. Point is, by learning to drive on the left side of the road and unlearning to drive on the right; it doesn't mean that you forgot how to drive on the right. Sometimes the hardest thing to do mentally is unlearning something and crucifying our ego. When we crucify the ego we open ourselves up to receive and develop a greater sense of internal and external awareness.

Emotions, Intent, and Manifestation

Thought and emotion is the foundation of manifestation and a key part in influencing your destiny. We cause so many things to occur in our lives and inadvertently off-set ourselves from our destined course. The Bible as well as numerous other ancient texts tells us that human beings have the power and the ability to speak things into existence if we only believe. Though this is true, there are still a lot of people that truly do not understand how to actually go about doing it. By going into detail of thought and emotion this will clarify and hopefully give a deeper meaning and understanding of the process of what manifestation is and how it actually works. Learning to control your emotions is key for that intended desire itself to manifest. If you let your emotions go unchecked the manifestation will never take place. This can be understood by having a clear understanding of Past-Present Relationships. Let's take a look at thoughts and emotions. Dr. Joe Dispenza explains this succinctly in his book "Becoming Supernatural" and you will begin to see that you are the catalyst of your own destiny. Every time you express a thought or an emotion there are a series or combination of different chemical chain reactions firing off inside of your body, in turn you physically feel the same way that you are thinking. Again, an example of how immaterial becomes material. If you are angry with another person, those angered thoughts will generate even more angered thoughts that are **equal** to how you feel. Now in turn, your thoughts are now thinking for your emotions and your emotions are thinking for your thoughts. Now you have two brains thinking at the same time and now you are stuck in a loop of thought and emotion. This is an example of a **Past, Present Relationship.**

You can simply think of a Past-Present Relationship like this: If someone disrespects you, Either knowingly or unknowingly, in that very moment you are brought back mentally or emotionally to a place where another person showed that same level of disrespect and when those angry emotions start to flare, you either see that same situation playing out again or you feel that same level of overwhelming emotion even if you can't remember in detail that past encounter exactly. Truthfully, it truly doesn't matter if you can remember it or not because it is at that very moment you put your entire state of being in the past. In that moment how you feel *is* your state of being. You are therefore no longer in the present moment emotionally. The key to controlling our emotions and preparing our body for manifestation is practicing being in the present moment. Your state of being must be in the present *now*. When you think of your failures and problems you are going through. When you first wake up in the morning you are starting your day, if you wake up thinking about your problems you are putting your entire state of being in the distant *past*. How? Because those life problems and those shortcomings are connected to the memories of your past experiences. If you are feeling sad, guilty, not worthy, depressed, fear, anger etc. Your thought process cannot operate on a higher frequency of thinking. The body only does what the mind tells it to do. Once your state of being is *in the present now* it is because you have opened yourself up and allowed your body to feel those high frequency emotions such as love, joy, happiness, gratitude etc.

The reason why that emotion has to be at a very high frequency is because that high frequency emotion is what latches onto the intent of the individual and acts as a bridge to bring it over to this three dimensional space for it to manifest. Stay with me. Whenever you don't know what emotion to feel, conjure the feeling of gratitude, because It is that unique feeling you get when something has already happened or something is about to happen. Remember that biblical scripture and other various ancient esoteric writings state that we must believe when trying to manifest? When the thoughts of that individual person comes from a very positive place, which are high frequency thoughts, and the individual makes their body literally feel that emotion, there is a connection created between thought and emotion. Thought is (mind) emotion is (body). This is exactly how you make both mind and body become one. As the old saying goes, "as above so below." When the mind and body becomes one the manifestation will take place. This process sets the ball in motion preparing that intent, that immaterial thought to be carried over to a three dimensional space to manifest itself.

Having negative emotions or feeling low vibratory feelings will not work even if you're thinking all positive thoughts. Simply, If you are feeling negative emotions those low vibratory feelings are far too weak to latch onto positive intentions and bring them over to a three dimensional space to manifest. If the mind is positive and the body is negative then there will remain to be a disconnect between the mind and the body. If the Mind has positive intentions of the future thought taking place and the body feels and believes its already in that future moment, then it is at that moment your entire state of being is in the future. The longer you can stay in that moment the more beneficial to you it will be. In the beginning of this chapter we talked about how we put our state of being in the past and now you just learned how to put it in the future.

Now that you know how to properly manifest it is also wise to understand that what you want to manifest isn't going to take place in the timing you may want it to take place. How quick it takes for your thought to manifest solely depends on how much energy you put out into the *aether*. Source allowed and granted us the power to speak into our existence not for us to decide when it will happen too. This makes perfect spiritual sense for a multitude of reasons. If the source of all things is omniscient and the human being we don't truly have a true understanding of time, why give us the ability to instantly make things manifest with our false sense of time? Secondly, the right thing at the wrong time and the wrong thing at the right time can set off a chain of events that can inadvertently cause a chain reaction and throw events and destinies off of their natural course. It's better to let someone or something that knows all and see all handle this part of the job. Edgar Cayce once said that it is best to ask God to bring things into our lives because a lot of times we lack the spiritual know how and we have a bad track record of conjuring the wrong things. We are truly infamous for conjuring the wrong things into our lives. Let's start with some basics. The secrets to manifestation to manifest positive things into our lives can broke down into three basic steps.

They are:

1. Positive Intent
2. High Frequency Emotion
3. Believe as if it has already happened/or feel the emotion ahead of the experience.

WARNING: Just like they say, be careful what you wish for. In this case ask for. Once you invoke the manifestation process things will go wrong and sideways before your desire is granted even if the desire is positive and well intentioned. The reason is because you spent the last several years doing wrong by people and decided to make a change overnight. All the things you have done up until the moment you decided to change, that energy has been building up. The moment that you decided to change things starts to happen opposite of what you desired to happen because that bad energy you put out, now it has to begin unraveling itself and prepare to be put somewhere new to start creating something new. During this unraveling, events may take place that you may perceive to be bad situations but the human brain is finite and it can't fully understand exactly what is happening spiritually but in actuality, it is only the universe doing its job as *Source* created it to do. Even if you feel you haven't done anything at all that is wrong, none of us have transcended karma yet so there is always something to answer for no matter how minor. In reality it's not just about good or bad. When you spend so much of your time putting your own energy towards unnecessary distractions such as; the bad relationships, television, cellphones, gangs, money, drugs, cars, clothes, jewelry, etc. You are siphoning energy off from yourself. Because that energy is flowing outward in every single direction; and because thoughts are energy, you are sending your thoughts and intent outward in every direction instead of flowing inward. When you are in the present moment you will let go of those distractions and your energy gets called back to you, Therefore, allowing it to untangle itself and preparing to create a new destiny.

How powerful is thought and can it really influence reality? Well, in 1986 there was a French Scientist by the name of Rene Peoc'h decided to do an experiment to see if thought or intent can influence objects or events. To keep track of all the data he built a R.E.G (Random Event Generator), and this is basically a computerized version of heads or tails that keeps track of all the probabilities of random events occurring that is different from what was originally intended. Dr. Peoc'h had decided to use a robot and baby chicks in order for this experiment to truly work. Peoc'h created a robot, programmed it to move 50 percent left and 50 percent right then placed it on a table. He first recorded the data without introducing the chicks and discovered that the robot had covered the table equally over time. Next Dr. Peoc'h introduced the unhatched chicks inside the cage to the robot by placing the chicks on the end of the table. Once the chicks hatched inside of the cage the first thing they saw was the moving robot and imprinted themselves onto the robot. In psychology the terminology "imprinting" is the phenomena in which a newborn being bonds with the first thing it meets at birth. If you know anything about baby chicks you know that they imprint or attach themselves to the first moving thing that they see because they believe that the moving thing is its mother. Once the chicks imprinted on the robot the cage was placed even further away from the robot making it even harder for them to get to. When placed further away the data showed that the robot no longer moved 50 percent left and 50 percent right but stayed toward the edge of the table and as close to the cage as it could possibly get. The chick's intentions to embrace and wanting to be close to the robot so much that the robot went against its program and closed the gap between itself and the chicks. One lesson to learn from this experiment is that it doesn't matter what you program yourself to do or react to. Your program can be re-written.

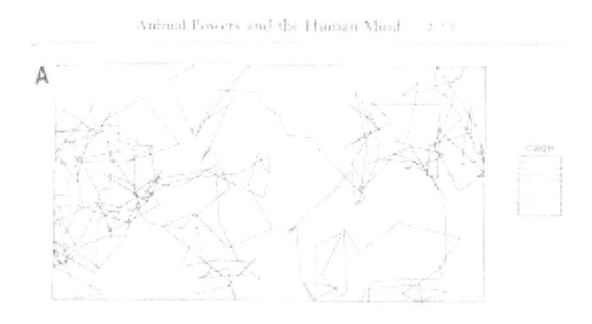

[Figure 9.1]

[Figure 9.2]

If Baby chicks have that much power inside of their small fragile bodies just imagine how much power you have locked inside of you waiting to be released. This experiment also showed how thoughts can influence electrical devices. Again, another example of how immaterial affects the material. We spend so much time on a daily basis focusing our energy on our outer world so much that we never really give that same level of energy and focus to our inner world. Imagine the unlimited possibilities of you putting and directing that same level of focus and concentrating that flow of energy inward.

Focusing our energy inward allows us to connect with our higher self, fostering spiritual growth and deeper self-awareness. From an esoteric perspective, this practice helps align our personal vibration with the universal energy, promoting harmony and inner peace. As we cultivate inner stillness, we access deeper levels of intuition and wisdom, thus enabling us to make choices that will lead to positive outcomes. This inward focus helps us to dissolve negative patterns and karmic influences, allowing for emotional healing and spiritual purification. By directing our energy inward, we strengthen our inner light, which radiates outward and positively affects the environment and people around us in our daily lives. It also fosters mental clarity and emotional resilience, helping us to navigate life's challenges with wisdom and grace. As we align with our soul's purpose, we manifest outcomes that are in harmony with our highest good.

Chapter 10: Gematria & Numerology

What is Gematria?

Gematria is a hidden esoteric method of using alphanumeric code of assigning a numerical value to a name, word or phrase according to its letters. It is an ancient Jewish form of numerology in which the various letters of the original Hebrew alphabet are more frequently substituted with their corresponding numbers. This ancient form of alphanumeric numerology is most commonly used to get a much deeper understanding from ancient spiritual texts such as the Bible and the Torah as well as other various ancient writings from other spiritual texts. The Holy Bible itself is completely and sacredly filled with countless hidden and highly advanced esoteric mathematical operations that sometimes contain some pretty simple coding that can very easily be deciphered that don't always require advanced numerological skillsets or techniques. Sometimes both the basic and the complex numerology in gematria are used to throw off an individual whom the information was never intended for. In ancient Greece, the Greeks called this ancient esoteric technique of coding **Isopsephy**, while practiced in ancient Hebrew, the Hebrews called it Gematria. Again, like before, as an example let's once again take a look at **Revelation 13:18** with a deeper insight this time

[18] *Here is wisdom. Let him that hath understanding count the number of the beast: for it is the number of a man; and his number is Six hundred threescore and six.*

We know that six hundred threescore and six is the same as **(666)**. That is the literal interpretation that we all understand because we live in a three dimensional reality and six hundred and sixty six is a number that is used in our number system in this three dimensional reality so that is why we understand it at first glance and that is fine. But what if I told you that you will have to multiply and add using this scripture? We will start by multiplying the scripture by the verse which will be **13x18** which will be **(13x18=234)** Now, we are about to see the deeper meaning behind most spiritual teachings. The numbers **234** and **432** are not just random numbers. They appear all throughout creation.

In the Biblical days, even in the renaissance period they will use what is called a "mirror image." They will write or draw a secret code and hold it up to a mirror and the hidden message will reveal itself. That is how they kept what was secret out of the hands of the Church. In this case the mirror of **234** is **432** and you will add **234** to its mirror which is **432**. So, in other words it will basically look something a lot like this. **(13x18=234) (243+432=666)**. This is one form of basic numerology to get the deeper meaning from spiritual texts. One example we see of gematria is the numerical value of *Satan* in Hebrew is **364**. Each letter is assigned a numerical value which adds up to give us **364**. It is said that Satan had the authority to persecute all of Israel for **364** days. Here we see what gematria actually is. It is a very well hidden esoteric system that uses both numbers and numerical values to show the relationships between words and phrases. Numbers and letters share a very close knit relationship that the average human mind wouldn't even know how to begin to process this advanced knowledge unless someone comes along and teaches it. Gematria has been used vastly during Biblical times and made its way down the worm hole of history into the present day. Its main purpose is to gain deeper insight into the interconnecting relationships of the various spiritual and physical concepts. Before we go any further I want you to know that you might have to go down a rabbit hole that you might not be used to, or learn concepts you've never been taught.

In other words, in order to get the full complex understanding and the deeper esoteric meaning behind this ancient teaching that we have come to call Gematria, or to begin to see the overwhelming evidence of interconnecting relationships between numbers, letters, and words you have to learn mysticism. At the very least learn some key concepts in mysticism. That is what we are about to dive into.

In chapter two we learned that there is energy in numbers and numbers can influence our reality or our three dimensional space. In chapter four we learned that words themselves, lines, and even symbols can also have the same effect upon reality the same as numbers. Let's take a look at how exactly we got twenty six letters in the English alphabet from a mysticism perspective to see just how the relationship of numbers and letters interconnect. We all know by now the historical understanding from what we were all taught in school, which is that English is a Latin language that was comprised from the twenty six letters in the Latin alphabet after the fall of the Roman Empire. Historically, yes this is True. However, what some teachers (don't) know is that the number twenty six was no accident by any means. The historical viewpoint never answers the question as to why twenty six letters were adopted in the first place especially when letters were continually added and then repeatedly removed from the English alphabet, and certainly at one point in time both English and Latin letters consisted of having up to thirty letters. So why exactly was twenty six the magic number? Majority of the credit of getting our English alphabet goes to the ancient Phoenicians. You got it, the early civilization mentioned in the Bible. In fact, there were several civilizations that had a strong influence including the ancient Babylonians as well as the ancient Egyptians with the creation of the alphabet. With the creation of the alphabet also came mysticism.

One of the earliest esoteric mystic teachings gave rise to what is known as "*Kabbalah*." The primary teaching in the Kabbalah is that God/*Source* had created everything in our physical creation with language by combining the numbers with the letter, with the word. That sounds complicated but soon it will all make sense to you. One of the earliest Jewish esoteric books on mysticism called **Sefer Yetzirah** which when translated means "The Book Of Creation" or "The Book Of Formation" literally states in the very first verse that God/*Source* created all things in our physical existence with three forms of expression which are Numbers, Letters and Words. If we cross reference with the Bible we see that it does in fact line up exactly with scripture. *Source spoke* the physical and the non-physical worlds into existence over a course of just six days and creation was complete in the [26th]verse. First hidden clue of the number twenty six reveals itself. Both the numbers six and twenty six are closely associated with both God and man. What do these numbers have to do with God/*Source* or man? You will see shortly.

In Hebrew the four letter name for God is written out as יהוה or translated into English as Yahweh. These four letter characters are known as the **Tetragrammaton**. Remember that Hebrew is read from the right to left. So written HWHY is how we would read it or perceive it originally but once written backwards, YHWH is then what it becomes. So if you were to write it in Hebrew, once those characters are written backwards they will then look like this הוהי. Remember that in gematria each individual letter is assigned a very specific numerical value based upon the numerical sequence that the individual letter is in, in the alphabet. To put it simply, look at it like this (י is the **10th** Hebrew letter, ה is the **5th** letter, ו is the **6th**, and ה is the **5th** again). So if you were to add the numerical values it will be written like this **10+5+6+5 = 26**. Make Sense? Now, if you think that all of this is just one big coincidence, let's use the English alphanumerical order and let's see what happens. In English (G is the **7th** letter, O is the **15th**, D is the **4th**). So God/*Source* is **(7+15+4 = 26)**. Here is where you can see the number twenty six intimately interconnected to the source of everything in our very existence. Not only is twenty six a number associated with God but the creation of man started in the twenty sixth verse. Moses was the author of the first five books including Genesis and he was born exactly twenty six generations after Adam.

Genesis 1:26

[26] ***Then God said, "Let us make mankind in our image, in our likeness, so that they may rule over the fish in the sea and the birds in the sky, over the livestock and all the wild animals, and over all the creatures that move along the ground."***

Earlier I had mentioned that you will begin to see the significance of both the number six and the number twenty six and what does it all mean being so interconnected with both God and Man. Take a look at **Genesis 1:26** and hopefully here is where it will all connect and make a lot more sense to you. We know that Adam was created in the twenty sixth verse but what if I told you that both the number twenty-six and six is also subsequently hidden within our very own anatomy as well? The human body is comprised of exactly **206** bones, both of our feet and ankles are both comprised of **26** bones a piece, we are all made from carbon, calcium, and bones which are all words that sums to **26**, carbon is the sixth element on the periodic table, carbon itself just as an element has **6** protons, **6** neutrons, and **6** electrons. Adam wasn't born, he was created. The same elements that created Adam are the same elements that make up every fiber of our being. There are four basic methods of calculating the value of a word as you are about to learn and two of those ways are easily grasped. For example: Think back to when I used the word [God] and the sum of each value equaled twenty six. To refresh your memory it looked like this.

(G is the **7th** letter, O is the **15th**, and D is the **4th** letter). So, **(7+15+4 = 26)**. Now that was only using the alphanumerical order of each individual letter. The second method is a step above. It's using the alphanumeric order plus incorporating numerology. In other words it will look like this. **(7+6+4=17)**. The reason is because **15** have two digits and it must be reduced to a single digit according to the rules of numerology. **(1+5=6)** and that is how we got six which had led to the overall sum being seventeen. **(7+6+4=17)**. Now that you understand those two basic methods now we can really get into the meat of it. So, in summary, gematria in Jewish mysticism is a multifaceted and very intricate system used for exploring the hidden meanings tucked within the Hebrew Scriptures. It adds a layer of both symbolic and numerical interpretation to the study of sacred texts, contributing to the rich tapestry of mystical traditions within Judaism. This practice, with variations in methods like **Standard Gematria**, **Ordinal Gematria**, and **Reduced Gematria**, allows both scholars and mystics alike to seek the connections and insights by examining words or phrases that share the same numerical value. Beyond its application to entire words, gematria also can extend to acronyms and phrases, enriching the vast interpretative landscape Integrated into the old Kabbalistic studies. Gematria often explores connections with the Tree of Life, thus emphasizing the symbolic significance of numbers. While some view gematria as a tool for personal reflection and practical applications, others approach it with skepticism. Despite its ancient origins, gematria has continued to be studied in modern times, adding a nuanced layer to the understanding of Hebrew Scriptures within the broader context of Jewish mysticism.

The use of Gematria was not all just about numerology but about accessing divine knowledge and understanding the nature of God. It provided insight into the connections between the material and the spiritual worlds, helping mystics to understand how the divine is manifested into the physical realm. This is one reason it became central to Kabbalistic thought. In modern times, Gematria continues to be of great interest to many of scholars, mystics, and spiritual seekers. Its methods have even been applied in modern Kabbalistic studies, numerology, and the New Age movement.

Hebrew Letter	Glyph	Ordinal	Reduction	Traditional
Aleph	א	1	1	1
Bet	ב	2	2	2
Gimel	ג	3	3	3
Daleth	ד	4	4	4
Heh	ה	5	5	5
Waw / Vav	ו	6	6	6
Zayin	ז	7	7	7
Het	ח	8	8	8
Tet	ט	9	9	9
Yod	י	10	1	10
Kaf	כ	11	2	20
Lamed	ל	12	3	30
Mem	מ	13	4	40
Nun	נ	14	5	50
Samech	ס	15	6	60
Ayin	ע	16	7	70
Peh	פ	17	8	80
Tzady	צ	18	9	90
Koof	ק	19	1	100
Reish	ר	20	2	200
Shin	ש	21	3	300
Taf	ת	22	4	400

[Figure 10.1]

If you take a look at the Hebrew Gematria chart you will notice that there are three primary variables that stand out. They are **Ordinal, Reduction,** and **Traditional**. **Ordinal** just simply means that it is the application of using the alphabetical order or system. **For Example**: So, if the first letter of the alphabet is Aleph and Taft is the last, then Aleph will of course be worth a value of **1** and Taft will be worth a value of **22**. **Reduction** is the application or technique of incorporating the rules of numerology and reducing any double digit to just one. So, if Yod has a number value of **10** then it will of course be reduced to **1** because **1+0=1**. **Traditional** is the most commonly used cipher technique that is used in Hebrew Gematria. For example, if Yod is a value of **10** then that is the value that will be used in the cipher in its original value. Let's break this down even further and more simplistically by giving a visual aid. Let's use the word "Kabbalah" as an example. In Hebrew form if we were to use the word קַבָּלָה or (Kabbalah) ordinal, reduction, and traditional will be broken down like this.

Hebrew Gematria

Ordinal: 19+2+12+15=38

Reduction: 1+2+3+5 = 11

Traditional: 100+2+30+5 = 137

English Gematria/English Ordinal

Ordinal: 11+1+2+2+1+12+1+8 = 38

Reduction: 2+1+2+2+1+3+1+8=20 (2+0)=2

A=1; B=2; C=3; D=4; E=5; F=6; G=7; H=8; I=9; J=10; K=11; L=12; M=13; N=14; O=15; P=16; Q=17; R=18; S=19; T=20; U=21; V=22; W=23; X=24; Y=25; Z=26

How will you know if your numbers are correct or aligned with its letters or words? Well for example if we use all three methods in Hebrew Gematria form and all three methods reduce to the same number you are correct. Example, in the ordinal method the sum was **38 (3+8=11) 1+1=2**. In the reduction method the sum was **11 (1+1=2)**. In the traditional method the sum was **137 (1+3+7=11) 1+1=2**. In the English Gematria form all sums still break down to the same single digit. This is how you cross check and know you are correct and have the correct values assigned.

There is another hidden esoteric method used in gematria known as Pythagorean Gematria. Reason is because Pythagoras believed the true numbers were 1 through 9. So in other words the letter J, the 10th letter, becomes **1** because **1+0=1**. The same method will be applied in Hebrew as well. Look at the Example Below.

Example

A=1; **B**=2; **C**=3; **D**=4; **E**=5; **F**=6; **G**=7; **H**=8; **I**=9; **J**=1; **K**=2; **L**=3; **M**=4; **N**=5; **O**=6; **P**=7; **Q**=8; **R**=9; **S**=1; **T**=2; **U**=3; **V**=4; **W**=5; **X**=6; **Y**=7; **Z**=8

A/J/S each equate to 1

B/K/T each equate to 2

C/L/U each equate to 35

D/M/V each equate to 4

E/N/W each equate to 5

F/O/X each equate to 6

G/P/Y each equate to 7

H/Q/Z each equate to 8

I/R each equate to 9

Using this new method, we will for example, use the word Kabbalah again and break down the numerical value to a single digit. The letter K, the **11th** letter, is worth **2** because **11 is 1+1 = 2**. You see, it completely doesn't matter which method you choose at all. When you break down the numerical value of the word to just a single digit, it will still have the very same numerology. Using the example of the word Kabbalah with K as **2**, the sum of **20 is 2+0 is 2**; and from decoding with K as **11**, the sum of 29 is 2+9 is **11**, and **11 is**

1+1 = 2. If you use the Ordinal method, the same still remains to be true; it will still reduce to the same single digit number every time.

Kabbalah = **2+1+2+2+1+3+1+8 = 20 (K is 2) 2+0=2**

Kabbalah = **11+1+2+2+1+3+1+8 = 29 (K is 11) 9+2=11 (1+1)=2**

We are going to stop right here. There are more concepts to this topic that go far beyond anything that we have discussed so far. I believe the basics of gematria are all broken down and given within this chapter and can start being applied at any time the next time you open your Bible, Torah, or any other spiritual book or text. You will get a deeper spiritual insight and a much broader perspective of creation and the intelligence behind it. Even words are also hidden in the Bible, not just numbers. If you take the first ten names of the Bible that are in **Genesis 5**, in the genealogy starting with Adam and ending with Noah, and translate them to English a hidden message appears. See [Figure 10.1]

Name	Meaning of Name
Adam	Man
Seth	appointed
Enosh	mortal
Kenan	sorrow
Mahalalel	the blessed God
Jared	shall come down
Enoch	teaching
Methuselah	His death shall bring
Lamech	the despairing
Noah	rest, comfort

[Figure 10.2]

If we rewrite the new hidden English translations the message will then read **Man (is) appointed mortal sorrow; (but) the Blessed God shall come down teaching (that) His death shall bring (the) despairing rest.**

Everything that *Source* does or will do is intentional. What is even more interesting is that the word has always existed and became flesh. This indicates that the first ten names were hidden all along as a prophecy that otherwise would have been impossible for just a mere human being to know without having divine intervention. Whether it is coded messages hidden in specific names or even clandestine numbers neatly tucked behind a scripture, those who are meant to find and decipher these codes are the ones who will change the world. *He who has eyes let him see.*

Interest in Bible codes surged in the 20th century, particularly with the publication of Michael Drosnin's 1997 book, The Bible Code, which claimed to have found predictions of modern events like the assassination of Yitzhak Rabin and 9/11 hidden in the text. Critics argue that such findings are the result of statistical anomalies, but proponents view them as evidence of divine encoding. The concept of Bible Codes, also known as Torah Codes, refers to the discovery of hidden messages within the Hebrew text of the Torah (the first five books of the Bible). Proponents believe that these messages can be revealed simply by using mathematical techniques such as **Equidistant Letter Sequences (ELS)**. In this method, letters are selected at very specific intervals to reveal words, phrases, or even prophecies that were otherwise concealed in the text. **Theomatics** is another modern system that is similar to Gematria that looks for numerical patterns in the Greek and Hebrew texts of the Bible. The term was coined by **Del Washburn**, who developed the method based on the premise that numbers in the Bible, such as the values of words and letters, carry significant divine messages. Theomatics attempts to show that there is in fact an intentional, mathematically encoded intelligent design within the Bible's text that confirms the divine authorship of the scriptures.

Chapter 11: Crystals

The Power of Crystals

I've decided to write this chapter on crystals because I noticed that when I wear my crystals out in the open, the questions I get asked the most is what is so special about crystals? Why does the color of the crystal even matter at all? What exactly are they? Or what is the deeper meaning of wearing a crystal in the first place? There is so much misinformation that's surrounding the use of crystals that this chapter will break it down and take all of the misinformation and mystery out of it. After the first wave of the Covid-19 pandemic, we see people's interest and the sales in books that were dealing with the esoteric, meditations, self-help and spirituality went way through the roof. That is including sales of people's newfound interest in crystals.

What is it about their majestic structures, their magical appearance that draws our human attention into them? Let's look to our history for a little understanding. The ancient Egyptian people as well as the Sumerians both used crystals in the ancient world. Crystals were also used in early India, China, and Mesopotamia for amulets and talismans. Well in fact, every advanced culture on the planet thousands of years ago didn't just utilize crystals in their civilization, but every advanced civilized culture during that time had exactly the same understanding and knowledge when it came to the utilization of crystals and they were separated by thousands of miles of ocean and land with little to no form of communication. Sometimes they would use crystals for healing and warding off negative energy, or oftentimes to even cause some kind of spiritual or supernatural phenomena to mysteriously occur. The average person refers to them as rocks but they are much more than rocks. A rock is any two or more minerals that have been bonded together, while a mineral is normally a naturally occurring inorganic element. A crystal, of course, refers to the organic makeup or the physical structure of that mineral, to put it simply, its atomic structure.

There are a multitude of different kinds of crystalline structures. A mineral can be part of a rock, and a crystal can be a mineral, but we use the term rock and crystal interchangeably to mean the same thing. As we had just learned, matter is 99.999999999999% empty space. Within all of that dark empty space is nothing but free flowing energy, frequency and of course vibration. We all have a frequency and therefore we all vibrate. As humans, our vibration is very unstable and so very easily influenced. Meaning our emotions, environment, friends, family, social media, bills and a wide multitude of other worldly distractions and stress can influence and violently disrupt our natural vibratory state which can cause our vibrations to change and fluctuate several times per day. While crystals on the other hand, efficiently maintain a very stable energy or vibratory signature that doesn't change quite as easily.

[Figure 11.1]

They are completely made up of a fixed, regularly repeating, and perfect geometric pattern of molecules and can also atomically maintain their natural state which is the complete and total opposite from our ever changing vibrations. This part here is very important information. You may ask yourself, why does it matter if the atoms or energy in a crystal are stable? The answer is the more stable the energy, the more powerful the affect that it has on the user and its environment, and very powerful energy signatures can influence the environment or other unstable energies around it like the human body because the human body has an invisible electromagnetic field. This is the reason why people wear crystals and sometimes say that they feel balanced or healed even if they don't know the science behind it. Crystals stabilize our energy signature because it is powerful enough to latch onto and interact with our own energy and bring it to equilibrium. Think of crystals as being an anchor for our energy field.

You see, the very origin of the root word **Occult** means "*hidden.*" Those that practice the occult, they practice influencing the natural laws or the natural forces that are already there but only (*hidden.*) To the public this knowledge is closely guarded and hidden and not easily accessible, nor to the average person are these spiritual laws known to exist. Utilizing this level of knowledge has never truly been openly known to the public. Knowledge that only a very select few groups or individuals have the privilege to know, or to be introduced to; in the wrong hands can bring either peace or chaos. Majority of this book can honestly be considered Occultism if we are going by the very definition because the majority of what is in this book is knowledge that is hidden and not readily or easily accessible to the public. *Some* of the occult practices are what some call *witchcraft*. What exactly is witchcraft you may ask? It is the invoking and/or the manipulation of what we know to be the *hidden,* natural unseen forces that are already present waiting to be tapped into. The same meaning as *occult* but simply called by a different name. Occult practices are not all about witchcraft or Harry Potter spells. Though witchcraft **CAN** be a part of the occult teachings, what separates witchcraft from other esoteric teachings is the intent of the individual person who practices it and the quality of energy that is involved.

A lot of what is taught in the occult teachings deals with sacred knowledge in various forms such as math, astrology, anatomy and science as well as the natural spiritual and physical laws and the influencing of those laws. See, if it wasn't for esoteric teachings or occult teachings long ago, then society or we as a people, will not be where we are today and we will not be as advanced nor living this comfortably. It is because of the occult mystic schools that were established thousands of years ago in Egypt, Greece and other places that allowed us to map the constellations and identify certain stars so that we can now safely and securely propel our brave astronauts to visiting other earth like worlds, or to give humanity a vast understanding of aerodynamics that led to the building of planes and other flying vehicles such as jets, helicopters, choppers and drones, and understanding the mathematics used that helped build and sustain our country's infrastructure. It is important to note that there are natural and spiritual laws that are outside of any man-made religion, because these laws and forces have always existed before the creation of any man and any man-made religion. For example, if there is power in the tongue, and I purposely try to make something, anything manifest within this physical three-dimensional reality, that desire which is immaterial, now becomes tangible. I therefore just influenced, manipulated, and invoked an unseen force to successfully reach and achieve a desired effect. The principal is the same.

When we go through trials and tribulations most of us invoke God the Father or Jesus the Son for divine guidance or some other god or deity depending on your belief system. The word *invoke* means to call on (a deity or spirit) in prayer, as a witness, or for inspiration, call earnestly for. When we pray, we are invoking, during church services we are invoking, when praying for the sick or for a person to be healed we are invoking, when praying for peace in the Middle

East we are invoking. Some of us spend so much of our time being afraid of what we don't understand and condemning the ones who have obtained the knowledge that we don't even realize we are doing the exact same thing as them but on a smaller scale. The only difference between the two, you just aren't consciously aware of it yet. A **Cult** is a relatively a very small group of people having religious beliefs or practices that's regarded by others as strange or sinister. Inside of a cult, just about anything can be worshiped, and anything can be called a god and usually, more often than not that idolizing and worshiping tends to truly be misplaced. Cults can also evolve into larger group members. If a group of people wake up one day and decide to worship a doorknob, then that door knob then becomes their god. That is the definition and example of a cult. The **Occult** on the other hand deals more with the hidden knowledge in mathematics, science, nature, astrology, anatomy and the overall application of that knowledge in creation, while cults deal more with the worshiping of gods, deities, and objects.

Now that we have cleared that up a little, let's get back to crystals. To be completely honest there is no definitive scientific research of crystals being able to heal, reflect or absorb human energy that has yet to be accepted in the mainstream community, but there are cases where we know that crystals indeed have mystical effects on the wearer. Science thousands of years later is still playing catch up to what some of us already knew for thousands of years. Crystals are known to work for those of us that use them by stimulating the chakra network, the energy points in our bodies that our very own chi or life energy flows through which are called meridians that lead to each of those points, as well as stimulating the astral body. If you are new to these spiritual concepts, you may have never heard of the term *astral body* before. The astral body or subtle body is the counterpart of the physical body. It might not make a lot of sense right now but more on the astral body and astral plane in a later chapter when we discuss astral projection.

The reason there isn't any concrete data in crystal healing is simple, think about it, if you take something like crystals which operate on a level which it can influence the spiritual, that is clearly on a level which there is no known scientific tool or device that exist that can test the profound effects that healing has on the human body. Therefore, the very notion to the average individual is that crystal healing doesn't exist because to that individual person it cannot be definitively proven inside a laboratory beyond a reasonable doubt. Honestly, we wouldn't even know where to begin to create such a device to measure something that our human finite brains don't fully understand. When it comes to energy crystals and their remarkable mystical healing properties don't, believe nor disbelieve, simply have our own experience.

How exactly do crystals get their amazing, mystical, supernatural power to influence a person's energetic signature or the energy of things in its nearby environment? It is often because of the massive amounts of energy and pressure from nature it took to form it. It nearly takes 1billion-3.3billion years to even create a diamond and millions to form crystals. Out of all the time passed in creation up until this moment you are reading this book, imagine all that energy that has been exerted, generated and stored in just a single mineral over all of these years. For a moment just imagine just how much pure and natural energy it takes simply forming just one diamond and one crystal. The boiling heat inside the earth's inner core is extremely hot, approximately **(9,392° Fahrenheit)**. That is on levels we couldn't even believe. From this intense heating and cooling of magma forms a much newer, a more pure element or substance, much like a diamond. A diamond is pure carbon. The human body is mostly made from carbon and because diamonds and crystals alike are naturally created, they naturally contain healing properties stored within them like the natural healing energy that comes from the sun and the moon. This all may seem like something out of a movie, but the ancients knew the amount of natural power in gems.

This intensified, more pure energetic material or element is now vibrating at a much higher frequency rate; in turn, influencing those energetic bodies including the astral body and other vibrations of objects and things in its local environment. Because the elements were formed in such a natural way with massive amounts of energy, when they vibrate at such a high frequency our energetic bodies absorb this high frequency energy. There are certain elements that have very beneficial results to the human body and can both purify and amplify our overall well-being. See the crystal itself isn't influencing the physical body by itself like many believe, but it is the energetic or astral body that heals the physical body because of the forces absorbed by the crystal. You just don't put a crystal on, and your physical body is magically in balance. It is the energetic body that communicates with the physical body which then allows for a gateway to be open which in turn allows the healing to take place. What happens in the spiritual will manifest in the physical. A lot of crystal collectors and wearers make the mistake of placing their focus solely on the crystal or giving power to the crystal as if the crystal by itself has the power when in truth; it is the creator, *Source* that is responsible for the creation and attributes of the crystal. It is okay to use crystals for their innate natural abilities, but one must be aware to not idolize them, or you will slip into that cult-like mindset where the object then becomes the idol or god.

Crystals are directly connected to the universal energy grid, a vast network of energy that encompasses all creation. Crystals act as amplifiers of this energy, capable of channeling higher vibrational frequencies from the cosmic realm into the physical world. This makes them tools for spiritual growth, healing, and communication with higher planes of existence. With crystals having a cosmic origin they are not just earthly minerals but are connected to the larger forces of creation including the stars. This gives them a very unique connection to both the earthly and celestial forces/energies, making them capable of bridging the gap between the physical and spiritual realms.

Activating Your Crystal

Let's discuss how to activate the stored potential energy from within a crystal. Let's say you find a buried crystal on a beach, or you may even purchase one out the store. How do you activate it? First you cleanse it, next, you charge it, and then program it. This might sound far-fetched and like a bunch of mumbo jumbo to you at first especially if you are new to this world of information but stick with me and I promise it will all come together. First you will cleanse the crystal after you find it or purchase it. There are several different ways to cleanse a crystal and the method of choice will solely be dependent on the personal taste of the wearer. One method of cleansing a crystal but not limited to, is to run water over it from a faucet or water source for approximately a minute. You can also place the crystal in a natural flowing stream, take a bowl of salt water [preferably sea salt or rock salt] and place the crystal inside or you can also take a bowl of uncooked brown rice and bury the crystal under the grains. If you haven't figured it out already, these methods remove any physical and spiritual impurities/energies from the crystal the same way a master swordsman will heat the iron to remove any impurities from the sword.

When a crystal is cleansed, what happens is the crystal can then vibrate at its natural frequency state. Think of how many hands and energies have either touched or been around the vicinity of the crystal which you now hold. You don't want to just pick up things and wear them on your body or just place them in your pocket without cleansing it first because again, human energy is again very unstable and there are too many factors that influence our thoughts, what and how we perceive events or experiences can influence how we feel throughout our day to day lives and energy does indeed attach itself to objects and people. When you begin the cleansing process and that crystal starts vibrating in its perfect state, because of the crystal's chemical makeup or its molecular structure, it can naturally hold its perfect balance state for quite some time, thus, rejecting the influences of outside forces or energies around or near it. So once the crystal starts vibrating at its optimal performance level, its perfect state, the human body and/or our energetic field will thus match those very same vibrations and frequency of that particular crystal. In scientific terminology this is what we call *entrainment*. **Entrainment** is the process in which one set of frequencies influences another set of frequencies and then those frequencies combine together thus creating one harmonious frequency. In psychology, to put it simply, entrainment refers to the adaptive function in which we synchronize our brains and bodies to the environment.

Step 2, you will want to charge your crystal. There are several ways to do this, and it will all be solely dependent on your taste or per the individual wearer. One of the simplest ways to actually do this is to bathe your crystal in sunlight or moonlight, I mean literally just let it sit or hang outdoors. I recommend no longer than four hours if you choose the sun method because too much exposure to the sun can damage the crystal and darken its color. Some crystals may even become brittle and then slowly begin to deteriorate. Again, this may sound like hocus pocus but keep following me, I promise we are going somewhere with all of this and it will all make sense. Now the average person may have never in their life even heard of charging crystals and will reject the very notion. Remember, all things are interconnected; you just need every piece to the puzzle to see the whole picture. So, in this second step, I believe a fair question some people may find themselves asking as they are reading and trying to understand this second step is, do the sun and moon contain properties that can potentially influence life or objects in nature? The answer is yes. Sunlight stimulates our bodies to produce what we know as vitamin d as well as stimulating the grass to adequately produce the food essential for the very survival of our green lawns that we see and walk onto every day, and it is also significantly vital in the production of chlorophyll. The gravitational pull of the moon is essential in creating an equilibrium in our oceans by the rising and falling of our tides, and the moon has also been utilized by some species for navigation as well as reproduction.

In this tech world that we live in today we are inevitably surrounded by technology; millions of devices being utilized, and all turned on at the same time. With all of these different devices in use that also means that there is a massive amount of radiation being emitted constantly. There are crystals out there like the black tourmaline that dissolves or rejects radiation. Not completely but to a significant degree to where it is less harmful to the individual. Black tourmaline is well known for having a very high concentration of iron within its structure and it can amplify the human body's natural magnetic field. Some other crystals have very high concentrations of iron and other kinds of various elements, and these known elements have purification properties very similar to how black tourmaline crystals reject harmful radiation. So you see, crystals have natural healing properties already in their molecular structure. When you start to understand what crystals contain, what healing or the beneficial property it has, you will then understand how to best use that crystal throughout your daily life or spiritual practice.

There is absolutely nothing negative or satanic about a naturally created organic mineral. Each crystal has its very own and unique individual property and its own individual power. Because crystals are naturally created from the earth itself, overtime, they naturally harness the energies from the sun and the moon. Because that energy has been infused inside of them over time, the individual person just has to have the knowledge of how to use that natural healing energy and use the crystal for its beneficial properties.

Step 3, now you program your crystal. You program your crystal by holding it in the palm of your hand and giving it a clear and specified instruction or directed high frequency emotion of intent. To put it simply, if you want your crystal to perform its natural function then instruct it to do so, if you want it to help manifest your goals into reality then instruct it and literally feel as if that goal has already happened or it's about to happen. Programming a crystal helps activate and unlock its natural properties and focus its energies specifically on your desires. Speaking your goals and desires to your crystals may seem a little weird, but by doing so you will then **imprint** your goals, your intentions, your desires, and all of your high frequency emotions into the crystal the same way the baby chicks had imprinted their desire to become closer to the robot into the robots programming as you learned in an earlier chapter. By now, if you made it this far along in this book as you have, I'm pretty confident that you understand thoughts influence reality. If you are still unsure about thoughts programming crystals and how strange it all might seem or even if you are still on the fence about it, allow me to introduce a more tangible perspective on the concept of crystals storing information. According to all the incredible research of Dr. Marcel Vogel, a former researcher and scientist for IBM, we know that crystals do in fact store information as well as transmit that information, and that information includes thoughts and emotions as well as the intentions of a person.

Vogel even conducted some of the most ingenious experiments that even showed human to plant communication and how plants can even feel things and read our thoughts. Not to mention Dr. Vogel has well over 100 patents to date under his name. Programming a crystal is very simple and easy. You don't have to be some guru, or a monk. Just say what you mean, mean what you say, and believe. Thoughts are information. Vogel's research suggested that thoughts are not merely intangible processes but rather have an energetic structure to them that can be imprinted onto crystals. He believed that thoughts create specific vibrational patterns, and when these patterns are directed toward a crystal, the crystal can "store" and "transmit" them. Crystals, being highly structured and vibrationally stable, can "remember" these thought patterns and radiate them back into the environment or toward a specific person or object. At this point in time, this line of innovating thinking wasn't popular nor in line with the direction the mainstream world was headed.

[Figure 11.2]   Marcel Vogel Crystal

When Vogel retired from rational science after twenty-seven years, he decided to walk, no, sprint into the spiritual realm, specifically holistic practices, which led to him creating the very infamous Vogel Crystal. Vogel realized early on that crystals can also be used to transmit the thoughts, emotions, and the intentions from the crystal holder to an individual person acting as the receiver. The more Vogel studied and practiced sending and receiving thoughts and emotions with crystals used as the medium, he decided to then use this knowledge for therapeutic purposes and also for healing. He learned that putting individuals in altered states of consciousness or a state of healing by sending life force energy or chi to a subject by simply using a directed thought. If you take a closer look at the Vogel crystal in [Figure 11.2] you may notice that its shape is one of the shapes used in sacred geometry, a hexagonal pattern. It takes patience, knowledge and understanding of sacred geometry and intersecting lines as you read in previous chapters is how the user is able to manipulate crystals. What do I mean? We'll, all energy whether it's energy from nature or your very own universal life force energy, [or chi] moves through the crystal in a directional motion being sent out or transmitted through the tip end of the crystal. Stay with me. When a crystal has a defined symmetrical structure like the six sided or twelve-sided hexagonal shape the energy is then gathered in the larger or wider part of the crystal and by thought or intent that energy is directed in a unidirectional path out the tip. When the tip of the crystal is congruent, perfectly centered with the C- axis or the lines that's running along the length of the crystal, the energy flowing outward is then amplified and more potent to the receiving subject. This ancient knowledge was utilized thousands upon thousands of years ago. We perceive it as merely impossible for the ancients to know all of this information during their time, but this really kind of makes you wonder, if they were considered this advanced back then, then what does that make us today?

[Figure 11.3] Marcel Vogel

Chapter 12:
Ley-Lines and Vortices

During the early 1920's a group of German dowsers noticed that some people were developing cancer in their homes at a very rapid rate. The dowsers were perplexed to see that their own neighbors weren't affected at all. When all the data from the dowsers were analyzed it was confirmed that underneath the houses of the people who developed cancer, there appeared to be water veins that were crisscrossing one above the other thus generating a vortexing or spiraling energy in the aetheric field which in turn, made a lot of random people sick. The trees growing above one of these energy centers will even grow into a twisted pattern. In 1921 an amateur archaeologist by the name of Alfred Watkins noticed that many of the ancient holy sites that we admire today are lined up in a straight line. He also believed that the early Christians located their holy sites by these energetic lines. Because of the incredible work of dowsers we now know that the earth has its very own energy grid and these ancient ley lines are a part of that grid. In case you are wondering what dowsing is, it is the practice of locating water and precious metals underground, as well as the ability to tell if there is a sudden change in energy in the surrounding environment simply by using two simple metal rods.

Scientists call this pseudoscience even though the ancients have been practicing this technique for thousands of years, but that's not really a surprise there. There are a couple types of energy grids and the most well-known of the few are called **The Curry Net** and **The Hartmann Net** which covers the entirety of mother earth. Some Native American Indian tribes used sacred geometry in combination with earth energies to direct earth energies around their homes and ceremonial structures that are known as *kivas*. Kivas function as a magnetic center, by simply drawing energy from the surrounding region and refocusing them out the kiva's upper center.

Labyrinths also have a role. A **labyrinth** is a two-dimensional maze with a single path. The specific kind of energy that's focused by the labyrinth maze is determined by its direction. The maze's esoteric role is two-fold; first is to gather the earth energies and the second is to guide the individual through the shapes pattern and tune them into the energies connected with that pattern.

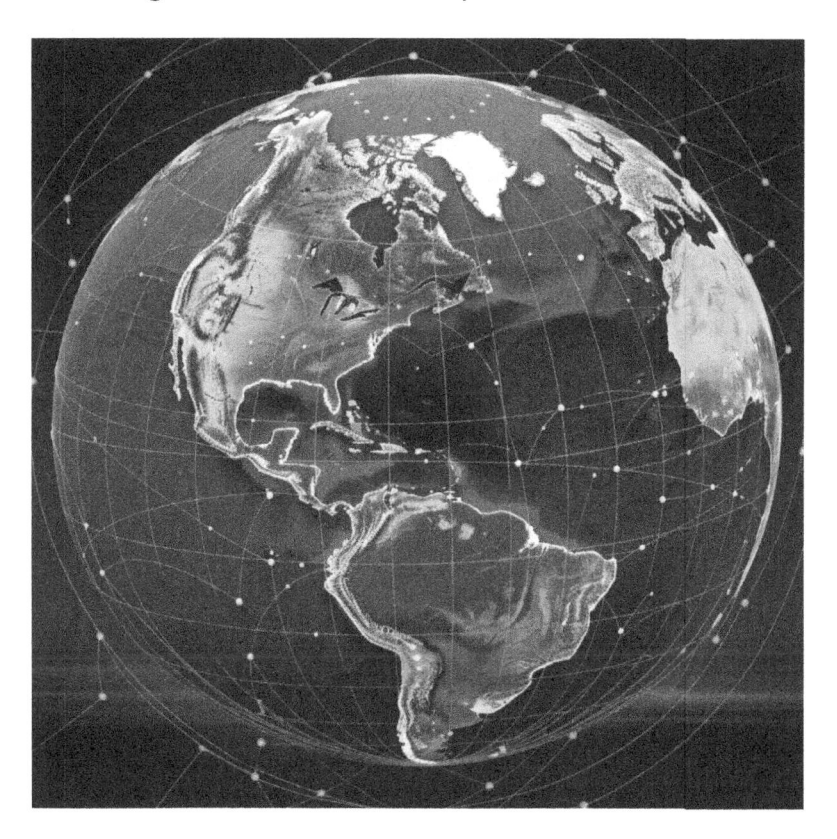

Figure 12.1

The Curry grid is stable and covers the entire earth. Their line runs approximately northeast-southwest to northwest-southeast direction and even continues to run at a diagonal to the latitude and longitude directions. It is even believed that the Curry Net is of earth origin. According to dowsers the lines are **10-12** feet apart in the northern and southern hemispheres and **12-15** feet apart as they get closer to the equator.

The Hartmann Net is also believed to run north-south/east-west. It is of cosmic origin and is not as stable as the Curry Net. Dowsers say that the Hartmann Net has these specific phase changes that occur at least four times a day: sunrise, noon, sunset, and midnight. Dan Davidson believes that during these phase changes, the grid disappears and seems to be influenced by cosmic or astrophysical activity such as phases of the moon, sunspot activity, and weather conditions. Davidson also has said that the east-west energetic grid lines intersect with the north-south grid lines and form vortices. He believes that depending on location and size of the grid line, the vortex can be either an ascending or descending motion of aetheric energy. These vortex points can either have negative or positive effects on our health.

The Cathie grid is very similar to the Hartmann Net. The Cathie grid is also entirely created of rectangles that are approximately 45 nautical miles square. Bruce Cathie believes the grid spacing is related to gravity, the speed of light, the mass of the entire earth and other natural earthy variables. Bruce Cathie's research shows overwhelming evidence that UFOs travel on this grid system. Regardless of your belief, when it comes to aliens and UFO's, between **1910 and 2015** alone there have been 80,000 reports of sightings. It also has been documented that some UFO crashes were traveling along this grid. Are extraterrestrials real? I'll let you decide. The 'creator gods' toured the area and changed the soil to correspond with significant roads called **'turingas,'** according to the **Australian Aborigines**. These 'turingas' are said to be revitalized at particular periods of the year by energies flowing through them, fertilizing the surrounding areas. They also claim that these wires can transmit messages across long distances. The ancient Incas had used the term "***Spirit-lines***" or in their language, are called "***ceques***." Ceques were described as sacred pathways. The ancient Indian word "ceqque" or "cheque" means boundary or line.

Vortices

What is a vortex? In science it is usually a mass of whirling fluid or air much like you see in a whirlpool or whirlwind. However, energy can also move in a vortex like motion. There are specific places on earth where energy is concentrated, and these charged energetic particles within a certain layer of earth's atmosphere are moving in a spiraling motion. It is how this energy is moving specifically that generates this concentrated energy. There are a total of twelve known vortices on earth that are all in a triangular shape. Most of everyone on the planet has come to know of the most mysterious, The Bermuda Triangle, but there are eleven more vortices that are around the world that produce the same unexplained phenomena. Earth's vortices are made up of the planet's natural electromagnetic field with very highly charged electrical particles that are moving in a spiraling formation, similar to the very movements of the chakras themselves. From the previous chapters you know that energy in motion has a frequency and therefore has a vibration. Vortices can intersect or align with nearby ley-lines. You may have also heard of these sacred sites across the world where mystical phenomena are well documented to occur, from **The Great Pyramids of Giza** in Egypt to **Stonehenge** in England or even **Chichén Itzá** in Mexico. As you've learned, spiraling or curves is feminine energy. So vortex energy coming into the earth is categorized as being female energy and the energy that is projected out of the earth is categorized as masculine energy. Around the world in some of these sacred sites, there are people taking advantage of some of the healing properties of being exposed to the immense energy signature that vortices emanate. We often hear a lot that people are disappearing around these energetic hotspots and instantly formulate in the back of our minds that vortices are bad and bad things will happen when we are in close proximity to one but there are pros to vortices. One thing science will unveil is that vortices are conductive to spiritual activity, especially with positive intent.

Note:

Vortices are very conducive to meditation as well as prayer and certain acoustic sounds and frequencies. There are two types of vortices, Planetary and Intentional. Planetary, is vortex energy created by our planet or by a celestial body. And Intentional, is when we have the intent of using energy to create or manifest something into our lives, we create a vortex of energy ourselves. Energy naturally moves in a spiraling vortex motion. Thoughts and emotions are also energy. So, the more we pray and meditate in repetition, the stronger the vortex energy that we create in our local space becomes.

These cultural sites or places that have vortex energy like **The Bermuda Triangle, The Dragons Triangle, The Alaska Triangle** etc. have all had dozens of reports of people, boats, ships, and planes disappearing. Loved ones just vanish into thin air with no trace at all. One thing scientists must be aware of is that the earth is a planetary body that is sitting in a nearly perfect vacuum that we call Outer-Space and each planetary body is subject to massive amounts of cosmic energy and cosmic forces that permeate through each of its planetary bodies including the earth. Where these cosmic energies build up is what we have identified as vortex hotspots because of their very unusual magnetic anomalies. When *Source* created physical existence, as you know there were forces sent or expressed outward from itself into the physical plane that we have observed on the physical plane, and gave those forces names such as gravity, magnetism, electricity and so forth. However, there are energies and forces that exist that science haven't discovered yet. In order for all of this to make more sense let me explain what magnetic flux is. A **Magnetic Flux** is simply a measurement of the total magnetic field that passes through a given area.

In other words, if you are flying in a plane and you fly over the Bermuda triangle, *[remember this is an area that has built up cosmic energy that God expressed outward that man hasn't discovered yet,]* and your compass and navigation equipment start to go haywire and begin to fail, that means there is a disturbance in the magnetic field. But that is just a fraction of the problem. These forces and energies that exist that we don't know exist, they have their own energetic fields as well and your equipment goes haywire as an indication that you are in the presence of these unknown energy fields. So yes, these vortex areas have magnetic anomalies because the magnetic field is bending, but these other forces and energies that we haven't discovered yet are introduced and are also bending along with the magnetic field. The equipment failure is just a symptom of what hasn't been discovered yet in motion.

Right before these airplane pilots, ship captains and crew members disappeared through these vortices, their vibrations would have been raised. Those who were on the threshold of crossing over into another space or dimension and survived to report and document it, stated that they had seen things and had spiritual and mystical experiences. Bermuda is not regarded as an earth vortex like the other vortices are but here are more sites in detail:

Sedona, Arizona, USA:

Sedona is often considered one of the primary vortex sites in the United States. It is infamous for its stunning red rock formations and it is widely believed to have multiple energy vortex locations there, including Boynton Canyon, Cathedral Rock, Bell Rock, and Airport Mesa. Visitors from everywhere have come to meditate, reflect, and experience the supposed healing energies of the area.

Mount Shasta, California, USA:

Mount Shasta, a dormant volcano in Northern California, is another popular vortex destination. It is mostly associated with spiritual and mystical beliefs, and some people believe it is home to a hidden city of advanced spiritual beings. The mountain's natural beauty and the perceived energy of the area draw those seeking spiritual growth.

Glastonbury, England:

Glastonbury is often referred to as the "Isle of Avalon." It is linked to Arthurian legend and has been considered a place of deep spiritual significance for centuries. Glastonbury Tor, a hill crowned by a medieval church tower, is believed to be an energy vortex. The town is known for its spiritual and New Age communities.

Machu Picchu, Peru:

Machu Picchu, an ancient Inca citadel high in the Andes Mountains, is admired for its stunning architecture and breathtaking location. Some believe it holds a spiritual energy vortex due to its historical and archaeological significance, as well as its remote and mystical atmosphere.

Mount Kailash, Tibet:

Mount Kailash, located in the Himalayas, is a sacred site in several Eastern religions, including Hinduism, Buddhism, and Jainism. It is believed to be the abode of deities and is associated with deep spiritual significance and pilgrimages.

Great Pyramids of Egypt:

The pyramids of Egypt, particularly the Great Pyramid of Giza, are considered by some to be energy vortices. These ancient structures have long held a fascination for their architectural and historical significance.

Stonehenge, England:

Stonehenge, a prehistoric stone circle, is associated with various mystical and spiritual beliefs. It's considered by some to be a place with unique energy or healing properties.

These locations often attract those individuals seeking personal transformation, spiritual experiences, and a deeper connection to the Earth and its history. While the scientific community does not support the idea of energy vortices as described in these beliefs, these sites continue to be popular destinations for those interested in deep spirituality, meditation, and the exploration of cultural and historical heritage.

People visit these spiritual places for various reasons, whether it's to connect with nature, explore the hidden mysteries of the past, or experience a sense of wonder and awe. The personal experiences and interpretations of these sites can be profoundly meaningful to those who visit them. Overall, the reasons for visiting sacred sites are very diverse and multifaceted, reflecting the complex interplay between religious, cultural, personal, and spiritual dimensions in the lives of individuals and communities.

Chapter 13:
The Human Aura

Understanding Aura

Take a moment to think, what comes to mind when you hear or think of the aura? Most of us will say that it is this invisible or sometimes visible glow of energy that surrounds the outline of a person or object, much like the beautiful glow around the moon when we look up on a dark cool night. Though this is true, it is only partially true. How the aura is created, and its primary functions are deeper and a little more complex than what most think. Earlier I had mentioned there are several subtle or energetic bodies within the physical body and the astral body was one of them as discussed. We will get into these subtle bodies but first understanding what the aura *is* and *how* the aura is made, will make the more complex information easier to understand later on because the foundation will be already laid. Buckle your seatbelt because this chapter will go into much greater detail and hopefully it will give a newfound understanding. There are several different ways to look at all the different concepts or perceptions of human aura when trying to get a concise understanding of what it actually is.

For those of us that took 5th grade earth science and for those of you who may have studied meteorology, you already know the earth itself has several different atmospheric layers within itself and that the five primary ones are the Troposphere, Stratosphere, Mesosphere, Thermosphere, and Exosphere. You also know that the earth has several layers going downward as well which are the Crust, Upper mantle, Mantle, Core, and Inner core. Just like the human body, the earth itself has both a material anatomy as well as an immaterial anatomy.

When an astronaut looks out of a rocket or the space station for the first time or even when we ourselves see a satellite image of our blue and green planet from a much more immaculate and much broader perspective we will see this beautiful blue hazy like glow or halo around our world and we describe this as earth's aura. We all have heard about those beautiful, dancing, energetic lights in the night sky at the northern and southern pole we all call the **Aurora Borealis** and the **Aurora Australis**. During either an aurora borealis or Aurora Australis light show, we are humbly witnessing a visible event that we categorize as a display of multi-colored auras. We see this majestic display of aura because solar winds are being ejected from the sun at very high speeds. Within these winds are electrically charged ionized particles and gas clouds. The earth's atmospheric layers also contain its very own gasses and charged particles. SolarWinds slam into our upper atmosphere at incredible speeds somewhere around 180-310 miles per second in all cardinal directions interacting and exciting these electrical charged particles in our atmosphere.

A question you may ask is why do we see different colors instead of just seeing one color? The answer is because there are a multitude of different gasses in the atmosphere made up from different atoms so therefore every time the sun ejects these electrically charged particles, whatever gas molecules it collides with and interacts with when it slams into our upper layer at high speed, this determines the color that will be displayed. That is how the aurora borealis and the Aurora Australis give us that surreal experience. It is said that some people can even hear the slamming of the energy during this majestic occurrence. The human energy field works in a very similar manner, constantly being shifted and influenced by both internal and external artifacts. Learning about aura which is also associated with light and color, can be very in depth subject to grasp at times.

[Figure 13.1]

How Aura is Created in Nature

We can better understand the very basics of the human aura by simply understanding a few basic necessary things. **Magnetism, magnetic field** and **electromagnetic field,** even what in the world is a **field** is to begin with. The earth itself generates a constant flow of electrical current and thus creates an electromagnetic field and that electromagnetic field or that generated field *is* the very *aura* itself. In fact, electricity and magnetic fields share a very close-knit relationship with the human aura. So, what is an electromagnetic field versus a magnetic field? *Electromagnetic fields* are created when there is both an active and constant flow of electrons or electric current around an electrically charged object. Stay with me. The definition of electromagnetic field simply means this:

Example: If you take a look at [figure 13.2] you will see that the battery has both a positive and negative side. The battery has an *active* and *constant* flow of current running from the battery to the wire wrapped around the nail. Because there is electricity flowing from the battery to the nail, the nail is then considered to be an electrically charged object. Now, since that nail is now receiving a constant flow of electrical current from the battery source it then produces an electromagnetic field around the coil thus becoming an electromagnet, and in turn, attracting the paperclips. Most of us have done this experiment in elementary school. Some of you may even remember doing it with a potato. In this example, this is called a **temporary magnet** because once you take away, disrupt or cut off the power source, then that electrically charged object will no longer have an electromagnetic field and therefore any nearby object can no longer be magnetized.

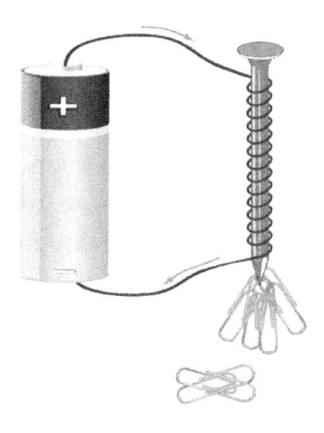

[Figure 13.2]

A **magnetic field** is the very field or region around a magnet that influences other magnetic objects that are nearby or within its field. **Magnetism** refers to the magnetic *properties* of objects that have the tendency to attract or repel each other. All of this can be much better understood by simply looking at a *permanent magnet*. Take a look at [figure 13.3]. If you take a white sheet of paper and placed a bar magnet or what some call a *permanent magnet* on top of that sheet, when you sprinkle iron filings around the magnet you will notice that the iron fillings will not only be attracted to the magnet but will organize or align themselves in a very specific pattern along what is call the *magnetic field lines*. Those visual magnetic field lines show the direction of the magnetic force at both ends of each pole on the magnet. The magnetic lines are used as visual tools to not only see the direction of the magnetic force, but it is also used as a visual tool to help see both the magnetic fields' strength and influence that it holds at or in a specific region or position in space. Magnetic fields are very special in magnets simply because of their natural atomic structure. The atoms are arranged in such a way that there are an equal amount of electrons that all move in the same direction which allows magnetism to occur. It is the movement that creates the force, and that force then creates a field. There are an equal number of electrons constantly moving in the same direction in magnets, that is very important information because in any other material or physical matter that we know in the universe as we have come to understand it, electrons move in opposite directions which cancels out magnetism in any other material object. That is the reason why there are certain materials such as paper, cloth, plastic etc. that can't be magnetized. There are other materials such as nickel, copper, iron, and even cobalt of course that have very strong magnetic properties because they have an equal amount of electrons that spin in the very same direction. All of this is a lot to take in but I promise it will all come together to give you a broader understanding.

Now even though nickel, iron, copper and cobalt, as well as several other materials are magnetic, that doesn't necessarily make them a **magnet**. To become **magnetized**, another strong magnetic material object must enter into the very same magnetic field of that existing magnet. Remember the magnetic field is the area or region around the magnet. Think of the magnetic field like a force field, much like what you will see in Star Wars or in Star Trek. Keeping that in mind should make it a little bit easier to grasp. Shortly ago I had briefly mentioned that in order to become magnetized, then another strong magnetic material object must enter the magnetic field of the existing magnet. Simply, if it can attract another similar material, then by definition you have a magnet. I just wanted to make that a bit clearer.

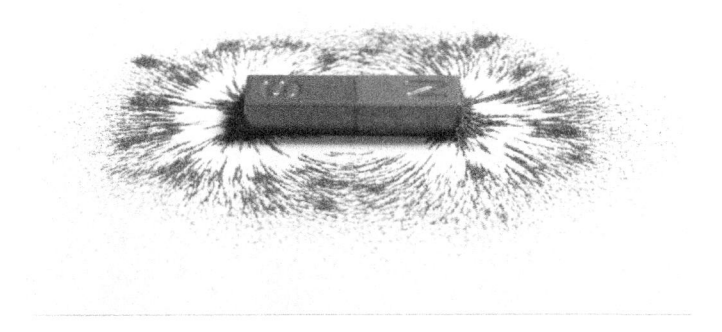

[Figure 13.3]

That also means that when something is magnetized it has the unique ability to induce or give magnetic properties to or can make another object magnetic. Take a closer look at [figure 13.4]. What that simply means is that if you had a soft metal iron bar [soft in this case, meaning malleable and that can easily be magnetized and demagnetized] as shown in [figure 13.4] and also had a permanent magnet like the one shown in [figure 13.3], If you take one pole of the permanent magnet and rubbed it straight up and down from one end of the bar to the other end, if you do this several times on both sides of the bar the bar will become magnetized through induction. This is called the **single *touch method***.

The method is believed to have been widely understood and utilized in some form for many centuries, but it became widely documented and studied in the 18th and 19th centuries, particularly during the development of electromagnetism. The scientific understanding of magnetism and the early development of these scientific methods were significantly influenced by early researchers such as William Gilbert, whose work De Magnete (1600) laid the foundation for the study of magnetism, and later figures like Hans Christian Orsted and André-Marie Ampère, who contributed to electromagnetism.

[Figure 13.4]

That was a lot of information so let's simplify everything learned so far. The primary difference between electromagnetic fields as seen in [figure 13.2] with the battery and the nail [which is man-made] and the natural magnetic fields created (naturally) as you seen in [Figure 13.3] with the bar magnet, is that an **electromagnetic field** is more specifically the relationship in which electricity interacts with a magnetic field. When there's an electric charge that's present that passes through a magnetized object like the iron nail, a magnetic field is thus created by the constant flowing of electrical current. It is electrically influenced, while a magnetic field can easily be created without an external electrical current.

magnetism is what we see as the physical phenomena, it refers to the magnetic properties of objects that have the tendency to attract or repel each other like the permanent magnet does naturally like as seen in [Figure 13.3] The simple difference that is between the two fields is the phenomena in which how the fields themselves occur or how they are created.

Let's use the earth as an example in a little bit more detail and apply all the knowledge just learned. In earth's outer core there is molten iron and nickel which generate a magnetic field. Well, from reading earlier in the chapter you know that both nickel and iron contain magnetic properties because the two elements have a natural atomic structure where the electrons are spinning in the very same direction which gives them their magnetic properties. This physical property as well as some known chemical properties is what allows earth to produce a *natural* magnetic field. So yes, earth is kind of like a permanent magnet itself. There is a catch though. Permanent magnetization as we have come to understand it cannot occur at temperatures above approximately **650° Celsius**. When converted to Fahrenheit that is around approximately **1,200° Fahrenheit**. According to the scientist over at National Geographic, earth's inner core is somewhere around **5,200° Celsius** which converted, is around **9,392° Fahrenheit**. The surface of the sun is a little over **10,000°Fahrenheit** so that gives a general idea of just how hot it can get. At extreme temperatures magnetization could not take place so therefore one will think that the earth does not have a magnetic field. Let's think back to earlier in this chapter where I explained a few ways to generate a magnetic field. Even though earth appears to lose its natural magnetic field due to the extreme temperatures, it makes it up by creating an electromagnetic field like the battery and nail method in [Figure 14.2]

Remember that electromagnetic fields are created from a moving electrical current. The inner core has molten liquid which are iron and nickel which have magnetic properties. It is literally liquid metal. So where does all this electricity come from? The electricity or *convection currents* are generated by both the vigorous motion and movement of the liquid metals inside the core combined with heat escaping from the core known as **Geodynamo**. To put it simply, heat and motion generates electricity under the right conditions. When all of those things have come together earth's protective electromagnetic field is then created. With all the information that you have read so far, I'm confident that you see the connection by now. See, whether you call it electromagnetic field or magnetic field. It is the field itself which is the aura. Not the quality of a person's mood as some will put into context when an individual steps into a room, but a literal, energetic energy field.

The Human Aura

With everything that you have learned so far about electricity, magnetism and magnetic fields, Let's digress for a moment and talk about boats and ships. It might seem like pointless information up until this point, but it will all come together. The more visuals and examples you are given the easier it will be to understand complex information. Stay with me. Some boats and ships will naturally generate electricity simply by moving along saltwater depending on what kind of metal the boat or ship is made from. The salt molecules that are in salt water are made of both sodium ions and chloride ions. Ions are simply atoms that have an electrical charge because they have either gained or lost an electron. Stay with me. This also means that they have both positive and negative charges. The water molecules pull the sodium and chlorine ions apart and in turn the positive and negative charges float freely on the water. This is what makes sea water highly conductive. Even when there is a ship or a boat that is completely stationary, the vessel still receives an electric charge because of the electric properties floating freely in the water. There are some cases where the electricity will eat away at the metal through a process called electrolysis. With where modern science is today that can be prevented. Your body behaves in very much the same manner as the boat and ship. See, the human body contains *trace metals*. You have **heavy metals** such as **mercury, lead, iron, chromium, arsenic, copper** etc. Then there is what is widely known as **trace metals** such as **iodine, zinc, iron, cobalt, nickel, manganese,** and **copper** again etc.

The difference between heavy and trace metals is that *heavy metals* are usually highly toxic at very low concentrations whereas *trace metals* are not toxic at low concentrations. Some trace metals can be heavy metals as you may have noticed in the elements I listed. Some trace and heavy metals contain correlating elements. That is because in very high concentrations trace metals are still toxic. Trace metals are the micronutrients your body needs for growth and development. If you will take a moment and look back at the list of trace metals, you will see that there are two elements the earth has in its core in high concentrations that gives it its electromagnetic field. If you remember what they are from what we discussed earlier, it will all start to come together because it's the same two elements found naturally inside the human body. They are iron and nickel. The human body is made mostly from water, these elements are moving through water, reacting, and producing electrical charges similar to how the hot liquid molten iron and nickel produce electrical charges while moving through the earth's inner core under very extreme temperatures and pressure or how the boats and ships course through an electrically charged liquid. Certain elements coming into contact with other elements as well as a number of chemical reactions constantly firing off in the body produces a very small electrical charge.

Though those electric charges can be extremely small they can still be detected by scientific instruments. These electrical charges are what produce or what gives the human body its aura, which is simply, an electromagnetic field. The brain alone isn't the only thing that produces electricity; the body does it as well. The human body is even a battery itself, an optimum source of renewable energy. Now that you understand a little more about the human aura and that it is an energetic or an electromagnetic field, and you know how it is produced, that information just doesn't stop there, because there are different layers of our aura, different layers of energetic bodies within the aura. From a holistic point of view aura is created by the different vibrational energies of the body. In biophysics, research into the our body's bio-field or bio-photon emissions, (light produced by living cells) some researchers suggest that subtle energy fields could play a role in cellular communication and overall well-being, though this field of study remains largely speculative in mainstream science today, it is a well-known truth amongst some.

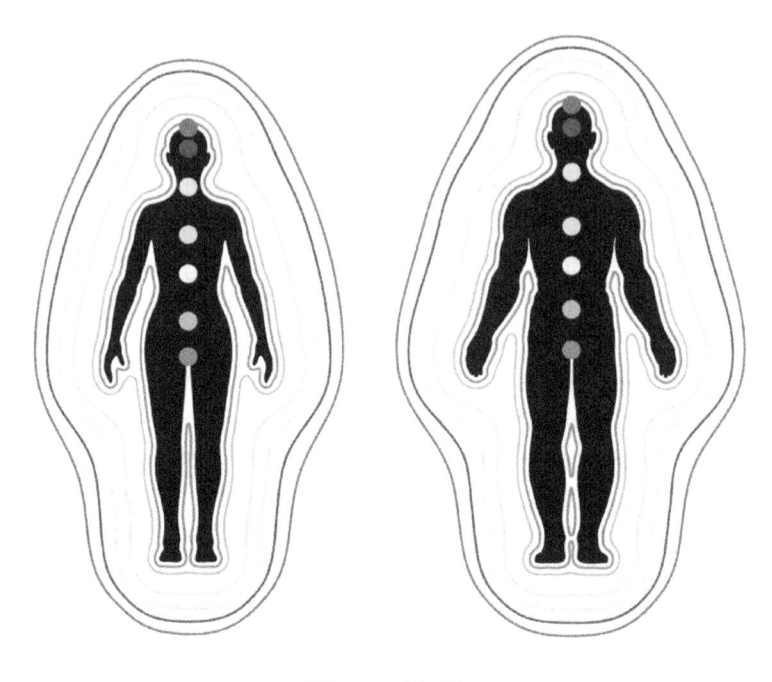

[Figure 13.5]

We all give off electromagnetic radiation. The magnetic field from our heart has been measured to expand outward up to three feet away and our brain waves which produce a much smaller field are measurable up to 1/10 of an inch from the skull. This is the reason why a person can step into a room and can feel the presence or emotions of others, at least those of us that are sensitive enough to feel auras. It is because our fields can expand outward. When we think of the human aura most of us don't know that an aura is like a fingerprint. How? Well, we perceive or think that within or around this energetic energy field is nothing but empty space. If quantum physics taught us anything by studying the electron is that all space contains information, and if there is something present, even if it's just information, then that means that all empty space isn't truly empty. We walk through infinite space everyday by moving from point A to point B. As we go about our daily activities, we don't realize that we are walking through so much radio waves and copious amounts of electrical signals that we can't see with the physical eye. All of those invisible signals that we are all walking through everyday contain vast amounts of information.

Aura is mostly represented by some people either as being one color or a multitude of ever-changing colors. Have you ever stopped and asked yourself what color actually is? What is it made of? How does it form in a way in which we can see it? Color is vibration, and if you think back to the very first chapter you will remember that all energy, frequency, and vibration contain and carry information. If you take a look at [figure 13.6] you will see that we only perceive the world, life, and everything in physical creation through a very small lens on the electromagnetic spectrum. When we give colors their name, we are simply naming the vibration or frequency of that waveform that we perceive as a specific color. To put it more simply, think of it more like this: There is a multitude of infinite colors, some of the most beautiful colors that we will never be able to perceive because they are beyond human perception. And because we don't have the ability to see some of these amazing colors outside of the visible light spectrum, those colors will never have a universally accepted name because we can't name something that we can't see. So, the name that we give to a specific color is just the name we give to a specific vibration.

The colors of your aura can show if you're sick, how sick, the mood that you're in during any given moment, if you are in pain, it can show the journey of your soul, show the overall physical, mental, and spiritual well-being. All these different variables are complexly encoded as high frequency information within the aura. Color is not just a sensory perception of light wavelengths but an expression of the vibrational nature of existence. This idea reflects the underlying principle that everything is connected through vibration, and color serves as a visible manifestation of this energetic spectrum.

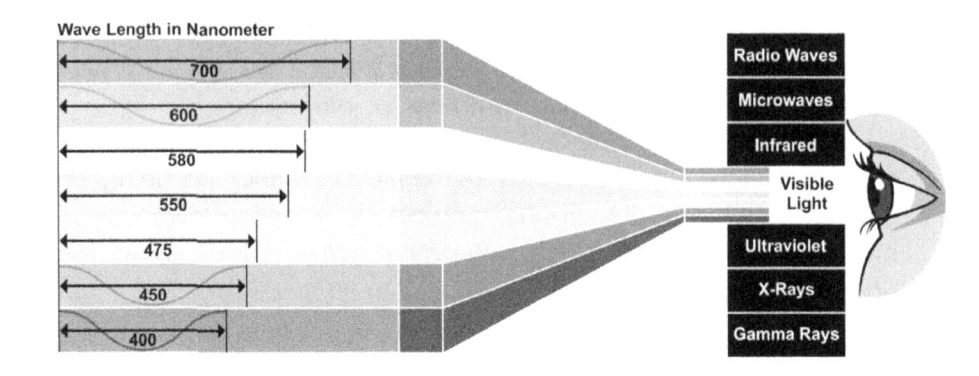

[Figure 13.6]

One thing people may not be aware of is that clothes or certain fabrics and materials can influence aura. If you are quick to anger or an overly aggressive person you might want to avoid red or certain shades of red. The clothes you wear can *clash* with aura. Just like the aura, sound is also vibrations. We operate every day hearing different sounds whether it's on the job, outdoors, or in our homes we hear sound everyday. Because we are so used to hearing sound everyday we also know that sometimes different sounds can clash and become disharmonic which we in the audio engineering field call dissonance. Examples of dissonance will be a baby crying, an alarm going off or even a random person giving off a high pitch scream. Any sound that is unpleasant to the human ear is considered to be disharmonic or dissonant. If you don't think the clothes you wear can clash with your aura, just think about this: If sound itself is created from vibrations and can clash and become disharmonic, then the very colors themselves which are essentially 'soundless' vibrations, can also clash and thus creating a spiritual disharmony. Be mindful of how certain colors make you feel and pay attention to how they affect your mood, emotions, and even our interactions with others. By us aligning our clothing choices with the energy of one's aura, a person can create a sense of inner harmony and balance.

The Subtle Bodies

If you ever took the time to really look and study different images of how artists or psychics draw auras around a person you will more often than not notice that the auras themselves are drawn in layers and they are always in the colors of the rainbow. These different layers we call subtle bodies or energetic bodies. What is their purpose, their function, their overall role and influence in our physical, mental and spiritual health and development? Depending on what part of the world you are in or what faith you are studying or practice, you may call these subtle bodies by different names and the number of them may be more or less than what we are about to discuss but we are going to look a few of these subtle bodies that directly correlate to the chakra system. In doing so, hopefully you will begin to understand just what the subtle bodies actually are, their primary purpose and function and realize no matter what spiritual practice that you are a part of, everything is interconnected. Each of these subtle energetic layered bodies can be looked at as different mediums for different qualities of energy and consciousness to express itself. As life force energy moves up the body through the chakra system this energy is still the same life force energy but just expressed in a different way. There is a book called **The Path of Emotions** by **Dr. Synthia Andrews**. In it she uses this very brilliant example of how to understand subtle energy by describing the close knit relationship between a fish and a fish tank. Imagine you have a fish inside a fish tank. The water is the medium in which the fish moves through. The water is the only thing that really connects the fish to everything else in its environment inside the tank. If you were to take your finger and place it inside the fish tank you will feel every move the fish makes through the vibrations of the water.

This is what is meant when describing how the subtle bodies act as a medium. Our thoughts, will, emotions, intent etc. all affect these different mediums everyday. When I use the term **express**, I simply mean it in the context of **being extracted, to show or come forth**. One might ask one very simple but yet very clever question as to why one individual person needs or projects that many layers of the human aura? The answer is simple. By now I am pretty confident that you have an in-depth understanding of chakras and the energy network. With that being said, this concept should be easy enough to understand once broken down. We know that the chakra network are wheels of spinning or spiraling energy at specific intersections of what we call chakra points. If there is energy in motion, spiraling, or just simply moving period, then there is something causing that movement. More importantly, with this constant continuous motion of these rotating spiraling chakras, there are also vast amounts of information being transmitted. Each chakra produces its own unique energy field, and this transmitted information is thus relayed to that corresponding aura field.

In other words, each individual chakra is responsible for transmitting information through to the aura from which each single one of them creates. We are all made up of unseen energy fields of information. Remember we are made from the very earth, just like the earth has different energy fields so does the human body. We won't go over all seven of the subtle bodies, but we will touch on a few of them just to get an understanding of how some of them operate and their functions. The energy bodies are not really "bodies" in the physical, material sense, but rather they are vibrational fields or subtle bodies that exist as a part of our overall multidimensional nature. Human beings possess multiple layers or levels of existence beyond just the physical body itself, which are often referred to as the "energy bodies" or "spiritual bodies". These energy bodies are integral to a person's overall well-being, influencing physical, emotional, mental, and spiritual health.

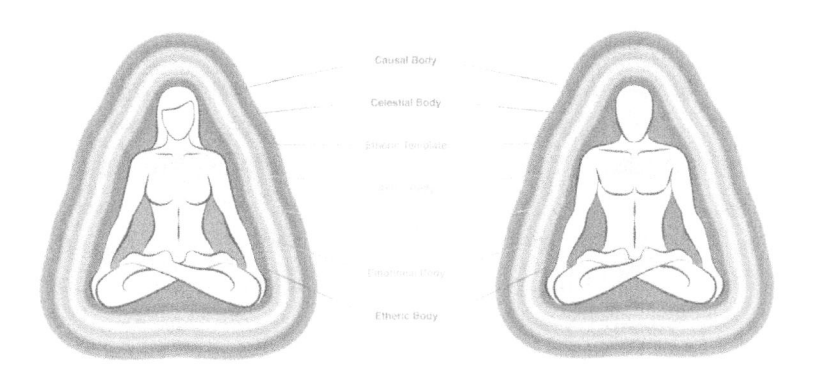

[Figure 13.7]

The first layer is the **Etheric Body**. This energy field is closest to the body and is about two inches from the skin. This field helps in physical consciousness. According to professor and American philosopher Ned Joel Block, the physical consciousness is a raw experience; moving, sounds and sensations etc. This is the energy field part of you that experiences physical reality. This energetic field is considered independent of any impact on behavior. The etheric field follows the exact contours around the human body, even enveloping the smallest mole or pimple. There is a weather phenomenon not popularly experienced or talked about or even known by most people that under the right conditions, can allow one to see the etheric field. This spooky phenomenon is called *Saint Elmo's fire*. It has been named after the famous Christian Saint, Saint Erasmus. This incandescent phenomenon typically occurs in stormy conditions, dry snow and ice crystals. It is when the air is highly ionized and in turn, causing a blue or purple-ish glow around certain points on a ship's masts or even certain points on an airplane. Saint Elmo's fire can also behave similar to lightning in how it discharges in the air leaving few confused with the notion that a lightning strike had taken place. The faint glow from Saint Elmo's fire is also very similar to the faint white or blue-ish glow one might see around electrical wires on a telephone pole on a dark night under the right conditions. When you hear stories about people who walked past graveyards at night and saw very faint energy rising up out from the ground, understand that what is being witnessed is that deceased body's etheric body. How so? It is simple. It is because that subtle etheric energy is now removing or detaching itself from a fresh decomposing corpse, even when that soul itself has already departed from the body. When the aura dies out from the human body, when a person dies the etheric body will sometimes remain for a while.

Example: If you were to put a pot on a stove and bring the water to a boil, the water will turn to steam and begin to evaporate. If the pot represents the body and the steam represents the etheric body then you can say as the pot which is the (Body) cools, [dies] the steam (etheric body) dissipates.

The etheric body can still linger well after the physical body is declared medically deceased even after the essence of life itself has disappeared from the physical body. The etheric body will wander about, and we call it the 'Ghost" because it will wander mindlessly. To put it simply, after death, trace amounts of etheric aura lingers, and this residual energy is how psychics are able to see or know who died. Most of us think that the moment a person dies, the moment life exits from the body, some of us believe that in that moment death is instantaneous. Death isn't quick. It's really quite a long and drawn-out process on levels beyond our three-dimensional perception. On a physical level we know death occurs in stages. After the brain dies, the organs will begin to die one by one followed by the hair and nails. Even though the physical body may die, there have been known instances where the aura of a medically deceased person can still be seen and will remain for several hours or several days. A person who is in excellent health might die violently, so that means if they are healthy during the time of their death and were in optimum health, their aura will remain fully charged. Think of it this way; when you plug your phone into the wall and that electrical current is giving the phone life, that cord now becomes the phone's lifeline so to speak. Once the phone reaches full capacity the charger or lifeline is removed from the phone. Once the lifeline or cord is removed, the phone still remains to keep its full charge even if it's dead or even if it breaks. Not only do a person's health or a violent act influences the strength and duration of the etheric aura but *fear* plays a significant role as well. People who die in a state of fear will leave behind a very strong etheric aura also. As stated earlier, this is the "**ghost**" or the "**phantom**" image of that person who has died and this etheric phantom image will continue to behave in the very same manner as if still inside the physical body.

Emotional Body is exactly what it is called. It is the emotional field. This energy field is how we all experience our very own thoughts and emotions. Emotions are projected and expressed through this energetic field, and we perceive that expression as sensations and feelings. Renowned and worldwide Author and spiritual teacher Teal Swan highlights that a feeling is not just an emotion, but a feeling is a sensation-based human perception, something that is immaterial in nature and that it converts itself into material to be experienced on the physical plane.

Mental Body The mental body is the energetic field or vehicle that is used simply for the expression of our thoughts, logic, memories, and reason. Thoughts or simply thinking itself is not from the activity of the brain, for the brain is only used to process and interpret it through the physical body. It is here in this energy field that the memories of our past lives lie dormant.

The astral body will be discussed in greater detail in the next chapter but I want to point out that each subtle or energetic body is connected to one another and each of these energetic bodies can be thought of as being the spiritual vehicles that is comprised of all the vital and essential components necessary; that are constantly expressing or manifesting themselves through our physical body on this three dimensional plane as a way for us or for our souls to experience all of this physical plane, to learn lessons through the souls experiences within this physical reality and transcend to a higher plane of existence as the end result. The energetic bodies convey information to the physical body on a deeper vibrational level. Just as the physical body itself is made up of dense physical matter, the spiritual components that make up these energetic spiritual bodies can be thought of in the same manner. In fact it is indeed matter, just a finer quality.

Chapter 14:
Astral Projection

Astral Projection Defined

To the average everyday person, astral projection might sound like a form of magic, or they may even associate it with the devil himself. You yourself may have heard the term used once or twice on an episode of charmed or your favorite TV show but in essence what is it truly? Astral Projection is what thousands if not millions of everyday regular people have reported and described in modern times as an (O.B.E) an Out of Body Experience. It is one of the subtle bodies or energetic bodies that co-exist within and alongside the physical body very similar to a Russian doll. A near death experience or sometimes called an (N.D.E) is known to trigger this mystical phenomenon but not limited to just an N.D.E. Again, it's very important to point out that near death experiences are *not* the only ways for us to induce this spiritual ability. Think in terms of a Russian doll, a doll within a doll, within another doll, within another doll, so on and so forth until you reach the smallest doll. If you are new to this concept or these ideas of astral projection you may be confused and ask how one body, be within or be inside of another body and completely reject the notion. The astral body can be very difficult to explain but most of you have heard of astral projection. Getting a solid understanding of the astral body can be much easier understood simply by looking at the spiritual phenomena we call astral projection. Think of it like this:

Example 1: The astral body as well as the physical body are almost sharing or occupying the very same position in space, only the astral body vibrates at a slightly different frequency then that of the physical body, just enough causing it to be in a different dimension but yet still totally aligned with the physical body, all while being simultaneously out of phase with it.

That may sound like a lot and confusing I know, or just think of it like this:

Example 2: You are traveling in your car listening to the radio, as soon as you cross over into the next town your radio is picking up the signal from another nearby station. Next thing you know, you begin to hear two radio stations playing at the same time. Those frequencies have a limit or range of how far they can reach or a set boundary. Once you cross over that boundary the next frequency starts fighting for space over the first frequency. For a moment both frequencies are sharing the same space but are out of phase with each other. If that example is too hard to grasp, let's break it down even further.

Example 3: Imagine you have two cups of water and both cups are filled to the top. In one cup you drop a spoon full of sand, and the water then begins to overflow out of the cup. The sand and the water can't occupy the same position in space because the sand is much heavier and forces the water to overflow. However, if you take several spoons of sugar and sprinkle it inside the second cup, the sugar molecules will dissolve, filling the spaces in between the water molecules allowing two things to share or occupy the same position in space. Astral projection can seem or is commonly spoken and taught as the soul leaving the body and though it can easily be perceived as the soul, I like to easily explain it as being a greater state of awareness. The individual person or the *projector* as we call them has projected themselves either by mistake or on purpose, will project a greater awareness or consciousness outside of, or beyond the physical body. The five senses is what allows your consciousness to have those physical experiences. As long as that consciousness continues to vibrate as closely tuned to a similar frequency as the body it will therefore continue to experience all of physical reality.

[Figure14.1]

Once consciousness is projected outside of the physical body, it now vibrates at a much higher frequency and is now on a plane of existence, dimension, or reality that is known as the astral plane, thus giving that individual a much greater state of higher awareness beyond the physical plane. Once in astral form, this higher state of awareness takes on a form known as the astral body. Just as your physical human body was perfectly created and designed as the perfect vehicle for the soul to have a physical or metaphysical experience; similarly the astral body is also a vehicle, the perfect spiritual vehicle which allows your higher state of consciousness to experience the astral world without having a material or a physical body. You're simply just an experience just having an experience. What I mean by that is when you astral project, your astral body is not bound by the same laws and restrictions as the physical body is restricted and limited to. So when you are in your astral form you don't necessarily need your five senses to fully experience the astral plane. In astral form, you can simply think of anywhere in the world or world(s), any planet, or any reality or dimension and be there within a blink of an eye with just a mere thought. There are a few more subtle bodies within the physical body and the astral body is just one layer. For the sake of understanding let's just focus on the astral body for now.

The Silver Cord

Only a few gifted people have seen this astral silver cord during their astral projection experience. Most people will not see the cord at all but that doesn't mean that it isn't there. So, what exactly is this silver cord? The silver cord or sometimes what is called "The Life Thread" is a silver-colored elastic cord that connects the astral body to the physical body, very similar to an umbilical cord. The silver cord is connected and runs through the other subtle bodies including the astral body and this cord is what is keeping the other energetic bodies tethered to the physical body. Because the astral self is pure consciousness and multiple things are a part of that consciousness including the soul, even the soul itself is also tethered to the chord because it is the chord that keeps the spiritual self-connected or tethered to the physical self. Think of it like this. When we think of an infant's umbilical cord, we all know that it is a physical object, tangible, visible, and of course something we can experience with the five senses. We know that its function is to provide nourishment to an unborn child and act as the primary conduit or medium between the unborn child and the placenta. Now, if the umbilical cord did not exist or by some random accident the umbilical cord somehow became severed, the unborn child will either never exist to begin with, or it wouldn't survive because its lifeline has been severed. The silver cord behaves in the very same manner and has the exact same function as the umbilical cord but on a spiritual level. Once the life thread or the silver cord is severed it is irreversible. See, when a person dies it is because that spiritual life thread, that silver cord is no longer connected to that individual's physical body. As a person is slowly dying those fine spiritual fibers that make up the cord slowly detach itself from the cord until it is no longer linked to the physical body.

Do you Understand now?

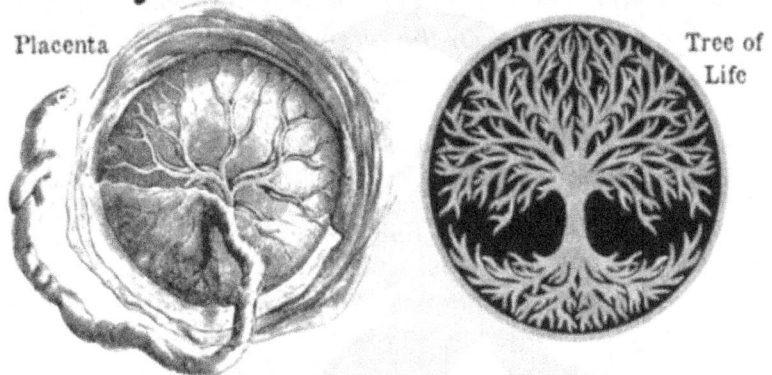

Placenta

Tree of Life

As the umbilical cord connects an unborn baby to the placenta so does the sivler cord connects our body with our spirit and thus the Divine Forces, the true Source of Life. When the umbilical cord is cut, we are born in this Realm. When the Silver cord is cut, we die and be reborn in another Realm.

umbilical cord

As Above So Below

silver cord

A wonderful Sivler Cord picture from Lobsang Rampa

Image from Lobsang Rampa [Figure 14.2]

The Bible speaks very briefly on the silver cord but it doesn't go into much further detail on the subject. The reason is, certain spiritual concepts and truths were understood at that time, so they didn't really need to be explained in extreme detail. If you take a look at **Ecclesiastes 12:6** it reads:

New King James Version

Ecclesiastes 12:6

Remember your Creator before the silver cord is loosed, Or the golden bowl is broken, Or the pitcher shattered at the fountain, Or the wheel broken at the well.

Here we see exactly where the silver cord is mentioned but most will not understand what exactly it's making a correlated reference to. In reality, this scripture is making a reference to several things with one being the intestines. However, what it's referring to on a much deeper esoteric understanding, is what we have come to know as the life thread or the silver-colored chord. The Bible chapter **Ecclesiastes 12:6** captures and highlights this divine silver cord perfectly. The same silver cord is also connected to what we all call in some spiritual circles as *ensoulment*. **Ensoulment** to put it simply is the very moment or the point in which a human gains its soul. Think back to what you learned earlier, we know that all souls come from and originate in Source or God. Therefore, if the soul is associated with life and already exists, then that will have to mean all life pre-exist long before incarnating as explained in an earlier chapter. So, at exactly what point does this ensoulment take place? In order to answer that question fully we first must understand three very important concepts. The first one is how a fetus or an embryo receives oxygen, the second is the creation of the silver cord itself, and the third is getting a precise understanding of what exactly is the soul.

One myth that we have to understand is that when we hear that unborn children in the womb can breathe in the same way we do on the outside and that is not true. When the mother of the unborn child takes a breath or inhales, that oxygen then travels through the lungs, into the heart, the vasculature, the uterus, and then into the placenta. Because the placenta is connected to the umbilical cord, oxygen can seamlessly flow from the placenta through the umbilical cord and into the unborn child allowing that newly unborn child to breathe. The second thing that we all must understand is that, as the physical body is being developed inside the womb, so are the spiritual bodies or the spiritual components, and that includes the silver cord. See, there is a spiritual anatomy just as well as there is a physical anatomy. As the physical body develops in its earliest stages, vast networks of energy pathways are formed for that new life force energy to start flowing through our body which are called *meridians*. During the physical development stage, this invisible development of spiritual meridians is literally simultaneous. There are vortices or spiraling energy centers that are also formed at very specific points throughout the human body during this spiritual development stage and these energy centers are then formed where meridians intersect. These newly formed energy centers at these cross sections are what we today call chakras.

The Soul

At what point does ensoulment take place? Remember ensoulment is the moment or point in which the soul enters the physical body. Let us break down precisely the true meaning of soul so that you may have a clear and concise understanding of what the soul actually is. **Genesis 2:7** reads**:** *And the Lord God formed man of the dust of the ground, and breathed into his nostrils the breath of life: and man became a living soul.* It is from this scripture that the answer is given to us as to what the soul actually is but most of us misinterpret it. The breath of life is *spirit* itself, the spirit contains life. The breath was infused with God's spirit. The word breath comes from both the Greek words **Pneuma** and the Hebrew word **Ruach** which both mean air/spirit. It is literally life force energy. After Adam was molded, he was simply just a shell, an empty sculpted corpse without life, until life, which was spirit, was introduced. The soul is that eternal aspect of an individual person that embodies all their personal experiences, emotions, thoughts, and consciousness. It is the very essence of a person's individuality and it evolves through various lifetimes. Therefore, the soul is not life. The breath of life was introduced and it was spirit that animated the body to become alive and thus Adam became a living personality, a living being, a living soul. Again, it is spirit that gives life to a physical body, not the soul. After the soul descends into the physical body, where does that life go once inside? It doesn't disappear, so where is it then housed? The answer to this question can be found two chapters over in **Leviticus 17:11**, and **verses 13-14**.

Leviticus 17:11

¹¹ For the life of the flesh is in the blood: and I have given it to you upon the altar to make an atonement for your souls: for it is the blood that maketh an atonement for the soul.

Leviticus 17:13-14

¹³ And whatsoever man there be of the children of Israel, or of the strangers that sojourn among you, which hunteth and catcheth any beast or fowl that may be eaten; he shall even pour out the blood thereof, and cover it with dust.

¹⁴ For it is the life of all flesh; the blood of it is for the life thereof: therefore I said unto the children of Israel, Ye shall eat the blood of no manner of flesh: for the life of all flesh is the blood thereof: whosoever eateth it shall be cut off.

The word *"soul"* is translated from the Hebrew word *"nephesh,"* that is then translated to **English** which means "*Life*." or "*Breath Of Life*" You probably caught on by now. See, if you look back at **Genesis 2:7** it tells us that the soul is that which was given life and became a living being, and if you read **Leviticus 17:11-14** it tells us that very same essence of life itself is in the blood of flesh., science today has the technology that shows that blood is indeed essential for life. That discovery is completely mind blowing and so well beyond ingenuous on behalf of the creator. It doesn't really matter what faith you practice, or who you may or may not believe in, I think any fair-minded person will look at this connection and can agree that this level of thought is far beyond anything a mere human can think of or let alone create this very complex system. I wonder how many others made this connection of life being literally in the blood?. Are there any other cultures out there that have made this connection as to the life force working in the blood? The answer is yes, the Hindus. In fact, they fill in the gap between the points in which the soul enters, and the point where the very essence of life starts to circulate through the blood which we will discuss shortly. Let's focus on what we know about blood itself. We know that without blood there is no life, we simply wouldn't survive. Blood transports oxygen to all of our vital organs, helps dispose of waste as well as numerous other functions. You may know that blood contains red blood cells and white blood cells but just think about that a little more deeply for a moment. Red and white blood cells are living cells, so if there are living cells within the blood then that means your blood is (*alive*). Life literally flows and circulates in us. This is the life force that is indeed necessary for the human body to function and to sustain us all in this life for us to experience this wonderful three-dimensional world that source has created for us, for as long as we are allowed. Without this infinite and eternal life seamlessly flowing throughout our bodies permeating every organ and fiber of our being we wouldn't even be able to move our bodies. I want to be absolutely clear, when I say that *spirit* is life, I'm not referring to that of the Holy Spirit. They are two different aspects.

You see, the spirit of an individual person is the eternal, divine part of their being, the aspect of themselves that is directly connected to God. It is the individual's true essence, transcending the physical body and all of the material world. It is divine in nature because every soul is part of the greater Whole (God), and the spirit of an individual is that which seeks to reunite with its Creator. The spirit is associated with a person's purpose and will, directing them toward spiritual growth and awakening. It is the overall driving force behind the soul's desire to align itself with higher principles such as love, kindness, and compassion. These basic things are just simply the qualities and attributes of the spirit. Now let me explain how the spirit is life. The **spirit** is the divine essence or the divine spark that animates and sustains life within each individual. It is the life force or the vital energy that originates from God and flows through every living being. The spirit is the very core of an individual's being, and it connects that individual person directly to the Creator. The spirit is the **personalized presence of God** within each and every individual person, meaning that while all spirits originate from the Divine, they are individualized in every human being. The spirit is the eternal, the immortal part of us that seeks union with God and reflects the soul's divine origin. **The Holy Spirit** is the **universal** and active force and manifestation of God's presence in the world. It is seen as the "**Comforter**" or Divine Presence that acts through creation, guiding and inspiring individuals toward the will of God. Unlike the personal spirit, the Holy Spirit is the universal, working throughout the universe to bring divine will into action. The Holy Spirit is the channel through which God's love, wisdom, and power flows into the world. It is that force that an individual attune to when seeking divine guidance or spiritual inspiration.

Key Differences:

Spirit: The individual spark, the divine essence within each person that serves as the connection or link between the soul and God. It is personal, eternal, and unique to each individual.

Holy Spirit: The universal, active manifestation of God's presence and power that works through creation to guide, comfort, and inspire. It is impersonal and operates on a broader, cosmic scale. One of the most significant roles of the Holy Spirit is that of the

Comforter, as described by Jesus in the New Testament (**John 14:16**). The Holy Spirit provides comfort, peace, and assurance to individuals during times of struggle or uncertainty. It serves as the spiritual guide in helping individuals to navigate life's challenges, offering inner strength, and finally then leading them to truth and understanding.

The Role in Spiritual Development: The individual's spirit is their inner connection to the divine, guiding them on their path of spiritual growth. The Holy Spirit acts as an external divine force that offers divine guidance, inspiration, and empowerment to align with higher purposes.

The human soul itself consists of several different attributes and/or components associated with it and which can be very difficult to understand at first. The combination of these different things makes up the soul in its totality. So what does that exactly mean? We are going to take this concept just a little deeper and look at the three components that make up the overall human being. Let us use the Bible as our reference and as a guide to get a more simplistic example and understanding of what the soul actually is. Hopefully, by doing this, the information that will come afterwards will be a little bit easier to consume.

1 Thessalonians 5:23

²³ May God himself, the God of peace, sanctify you through and through. May your whole spirit, soul and body be kept blameless at the coming of our Lord Jesus Christ.

Here we see that we are all created in three parts which are spirit, soul, and body. In order for us to see the whole picture, let us first dissect each part. We know that the **physical body** is the material, the matter in which we are made of. It contains both internal and external organs and it is also what houses the soul. The **spirit** is what is used as a channel of **communication** that serves as a link to communicate with Source/God or the entity the individual person worships. This divine spiritual link doesn't just serve as a channel of communication but also as a way for the individual person to overall experience the presence and love from the source of all creation and it is also how the individual rejoices in source or show thanks, appreciation, or gratitude. In the Bible, every time someone, I mean anyone, had experienced the presence of God or had a spiritual encounter, it was always with and through the spirit and not with or through the soul. The reason this is happening is because the world and material things influence the soul, but the spirit remains in its original state with only one purpose. The human **soul** is simply the personality aspect of the individual. It is much more than that but we will go much further in depth on the soul later. The soul acts as the bridge to the spirit and just that aspect or function of it alone can become confusing. That is why most people solely think of it as just the personality but it is so much more than that.

Luke 1:46-47 *"And Mary said, "My soul magnifies the Lord, and my spirit rejoices in God my Savior,"* **This is key to point out because this scripture shows a separation between the soul and the spirit. Secondly, the reason why Mary's soul magnifies the lord and not the spirit is because emotion is connected to the soul and not the spirit.** Galatians 5:16-17 *"But I say, walk by the Spirit, and you will not gratify the desires of the flesh. For the desires of the flesh are against the Spirit, and the desires of the Spirit are against the flesh, for these are opposed to each other, to keep you from doing the things you want to do."* **I will explain this scripture shortly, so for the sake of easy comprehension let us move on to the soul.**

As mentioned just shortly ago, the **soul** is composed of several different things [but not limited to] such as the mind, will, ego, intellect, desire, and emotions. It is the combination of these things which makes up the totality of the soul. All of these components influence the flesh because all of these components are influenced by the world. Think of the soul in the context as being the true self, the total personality, and the things listed just a few sentences ago are the things that make up that total personality. The mind is related to the soul according to **Proverbs 2:10** which says that **"Wisdom will enter your heart and knowledge will be pleasant to your soul."** Remember knowledge is a matter of the mind not the brain, and the mind not the brain is part of the soul.

Proverbs 24:14 [14] **So shall the knowledge of wisdom be unto thy soul: when thou hast found it, then there shall be a reward, and thy expectation shall not be cut off**, clearly shows that knowledge as well as wisdom are associated with being part of the soul. Now, let's take a look back at **Galatians 5:16-17** and let's try to break it down just a little further. The scripture is highlighting the mind, emotions and desires which are all things that influence the soul. Let us focus on the mind and the soul relationship because most of us say that we are composed of mind, body and soul not understanding the mind is just one layer or simply just one Russian doll encased in another. I feel that it is very important to point out this tight knitted mind and soul relationship. If you **read Galatians 5:16-17** carefully, you will begin to understand that the mind is what perceives, it has the ability to receive and interpret information. The five senses are also connected to the mind as well. It helps communicate with the body to perceive what is going on around it and therefore the mind is within the soul. Why is it the soul so easily influenced?

To put it simply, look at it like this:

When Source created Adam, Adam was created from the earth. The mind perceives and interprets all of life and its experiences which then inadvertently influences and feeds our emotions, our ego, our desires, and our intellect, etc. The soul is influenced by the mind; the mind glorifies earthly possessions, and material desires become an obsession, the ego looks for acceptance, and these are the things that will make up and influence the human soul. Our personality, thoughts, our emotions, desires, our will, our ego, are all part of the soul. These things change constantly because we largely come from and are part of earth. What do I mean by that exactly? Well, the reason why our outside environment changes these attributes and qualities about us is because the earth itself goes through constant shifts and changes, and we all are made from the very same material as the earth.

Everything that has ever been created or has come from the earth goes through changes. This is why living through the soul, living by only what you can feel or experience with the five senses is not good because you are living by things that change and shift from day to day. When you live your life through the spirit, you are not living life or operating out of complete randomness but complete order. When you live through the spirit, your eyes are open, and you develop a visual prowess that allows you to see what and who is not placed into your life for your own spiritual growth. The soul is a direct part of the Creator. The soul is closely linked to the mind which bridges together the material and spiritual realms. The mind acts as a spiritual tool through which the soul expresses itself in the physical world. The soul has free will, enabling it to make choices, learn, and then evolve. This free will is very essential in shaping its journey through lifetimes. The soul carries all of its experiences, memories, and all of its lessons from previous incarnations. These experiences can influence the current life and the soul's spiritual progression.

Ensoulment

The moment the soul enters the body, can either be at conception, any time frame during the pregnancy, or even during the delivery when the child is delivered and takes its first breath. As a side note, most think conception is when the newborn is delivered. When most people hear of conception, they believe it is at the point during birth, when the child is physically delivered or the point at which the child is guided out through the opening of the birth canal. That is entirely wrong. Let us think back to tenth grade Biology. Conception can take anywhere from a few minutes, to a few days, even a few weeks, and it occurs the moment the sperm meets the egg deep inside the Fallopian tubes. Most people will think that everything happens inside the uterus, that's not entirely true either. Once the sperm cell meets the egg cell, now this fertilized egg buries or implants itself within the lining of the uterine wall which is called *implantation*. During this entire process from once the sperm is introduced, up until between **8-10 weeks**, the unborn child then goes through what is called a **germinal *stage*** two weeks after conception takes place. The third week to around the ninth or tenth week, it's now an embryo. This period is called the **embryonic period**. It isn't until between the eighth to tenth week the unborn child becomes a fetus. Yes, there is a slight difference between the embryo and a fetus. Why is this very important for you to know? Because it will help you understand the moment ensoulment takes place. In some cultures in the world the women are trained to sense when the soul enters the unborn child. When a mother feels the kick of her unborn child for the first time it is believed that at that precise moment the soul had just entered their physical body.

Now, here's the Hindu connection. Remember earlier in the chapter we learned that the soul itself is the carrier of life, and not the life force itself, and once that life enters into the physical body it then flows throughout the blood animating every cell. According to the Hindus, on the top of the head of an unborn fetus, there is a spot known as **Brahmarandhra**, and **randhra,** translated to *"passage."* If you ever notice, once a child is born there is a tender spot on the crown of the Child's head. There is no bone at all in that occipital area, just muscle, which is why it feels tender. This is where the soul is said to descend down into the child when it is still a fetus. The sole reason the soul descends into the fetus versus during the embryonic period, is simply because the fetus contains the proper development to receive that soul. It's important to point out that this area of the skull is also a chakra energy center. This seamless flow of divine motion makes spiritual sense that a soul which is made of energy, will enter through an energy center and not from any other place either on or in the body. When the heart and brain developed enough and the spiritual passage has opened enough to receive an incoming soul, the soul will descend down into the physical body. Mind you, the soul is a spiritual/divine essence and **spirit** moves perfectly and in order, so a soul just won't randomly descend into a physical body without it first being the appropriate time or without the physical body being developed enough to receive it.

Think of it like this: If you walked into an electronic store and you say, unknowingly bought a faulty electrical device, let's say a phone and you then take that phone home. In excitement you take the phone out of the box and plug the phone into its charger and place it in the socket. The very moment you apply an electrical current to the phone, the phone will explode. Reason being is that the phone's internal system was never properly developed or well equipped to handle that kind of power flowing through it all coming from that incoming electrical current.

The very same thing goes for the process of the soul entering into a physical vessel. A small window of opportunity opens up for the soul to then descend into the physical vessel of that unborn fetus because that is the very moment when the proper brain and heart formation or the electric circuits has had enough time to form and a spiritual *passage*way has developed or matured stable enough to open and thus receiving the incoming soul. A soul in essence is a divine energy that has infinite consciousness, and its very essence is eternal, the soul will never truly die. If that kind of spiritual power [electricity] is introduced into a vessel [faulty device] before it is ready, the vessel wouldn't survive. This is why the precise timing of the soul's descent is important. It is also believed that once the soul descends into the physical body the soul takes its place in the heart because the heart is the first organ to appear or be created. The soul then acts as a tree, branching outwards and reaching the brain and eventually the entire body flowing life into the bloodstream. So the soul is everywhere inside of you and nowhere at the same time.

The heart is what appears first in the embryogenesis stage or in embryonic development. According to our top Neuroscientists, the human brain isn't fully developed until around the average age of twenty-five. Simply from a functionality standpoint, once the embryo is big enough or reaches a size that it can no longer adequately obtain enough surviving oxygen by the process known medically as **oxygen diffusion**, which is a secondary backup circulatory system then kicks in and takes its place to help distribute it. A developing embryo can't suffice the oxygen supply that is needed nor the basic nutritional requirements needed from just the maternal circulation alone. One may have a very hard time believing that at any point in the womb a fetus is soulless until it receives its soul and deem it as impossible for the fetus or embryo to be alive. However, it is the life force of the mother that acts as a conduit and what is shared with the unborn child though the child doesn't yet have a personality or soul.

Some of you may have heard through your spiritual journey that the pineal gland also called "**The Third Eye**" is the seat of the soul while others say that it is the pituitary gland or the heart as you just read. I will explain why these are said to be the seat of the soul shortly. All three of these parts of the body are interconnected. Let's start by looking more deeply at the heart. The heart is a mysterious organ because at one point in time we believed that the brain was the dominant force in our biological makeup. The heart is what we now call an auto rhythmic organ which just simply means we now know that it functions independently from the brain. There have been several experiments done where the heart will be removed completely from an unresponsive body and placed inside a solution called "**Ringer's Solution**" where the heart will continue to beat without a stimulated connection to the brain. As you read earlier, even the heart beats before the actual brain is formed. You see, the heart and brain are connected by sensory neurons that carry nerve impulses from sensory stimuli all while still allowing the heart to keep its independence separate from the physical brain. Many ancient civilizations believed that the heart was and still is the center of life in the human body. Before the birth of Christianity and its recognition as a legalized religion by Emperor Constantine, the ancient Greeks as well as a multitude of other ancient cultures recognized the heart as being the center of the soul. Thanks to the gigantic leap in our science and technology these past **2,000** years scientists are now just beginning to finally understand what mystics and spiritualists have been saying for several centuries. The heart generates magnetic fields and thus can help us to connect to our higher states of awareness by tapping into the quantum field. Its function goes beyond just sustaining our life. The very heart itself sits at an energy center or meridian cross section we call the heart chakra. There are three primary energy centers sitting below the heart and three primary energy centers above the heart which represents the earthly bodies and our higher self and therefore puts the heart dead center surrounded above and below these energy centers we come to know as the seven primary chakras.

If you read this far, by now you know both *how* and *when* the soul enters the human body. According to the extensive works of both Edgar Cayce and Dolores Cannon, as stated earlier, remember that a soul can enter a physical body at **any given time frame**. This time frame again, can be anywhere from **conception, during the pregnancy stage, when the newborn takes its first breath** or **shortly after the birth has taken place**. But even so, that time frame has a very limited window. A human soul deciding to take on the responsibility of having a physical body is a gradual process. It's not like when a person gets pregnant and a soul jumps at the first opportunity, or it is as easy as putting on a Halloween costume. The right conditions must be met. Every soul has the free will to decide if it wants to experience the physical world, and it can use its free will to choose exactly what part of incarnating into life that it wants to experience. It can be all of it, just part of it, or even none of it at all.

During a partial entry, for some, the soul may simply "hover" or "attach" to the developing fetus during pregnancy, but still not fully integrated with the body, not even during the gestation process. This suggests that the soul can observe or influence the physical body without being fully present. If it's a late entry, then in some cases, the soul may not fully enter the body until after birth. For example, the soul might wait to enter once the baby takes its first breath, linking the entry to a very significant moment of physical life, or according to Cayce, the latest being within seven to ten days after birth. The soul fully integrating with its body is a slow merge.

The soul can constantly move in and out of the fetus experiencing different perspectives of its earthly development. Though it can move in and out between both the spiritual and physical worlds, at no time is the soul fully integrated and fully locked in with its potential future physical body. It is anytime within this seven to ten day period after the newborn's birth in which the full connection between the spiritual and physical becomes fully established. This grace period of seven to ten days, allows the body and spirit to align and to be in complete harmony with each other. During this time, the physical body becomes more attuned to the soul's energy, and the soul then prepares to take on the full responsibility of its earthly journey. The soul of course still retains its free will and at some point may even decide during these first few days whether it will stay and fully inhabit the body, withdraw if the conditions aren't right, or the karmic or spiritual purposes have been fulfilled. In this sense, the soul is still making a final decision about its incarnation. However, if the soul still doesn't decide to fully integrate during this period, it can then result in what is known as "Crib Death". As of currently, there is no medical explanation for crib deaths, or what is known medically as Sudden Infant Death Syndrome. (S.I.D.S). When it comes to what is known as a **stillbirth**, it can be caused by placental problems, infection, birth defects, umbilical issues etc. In many cases, there is no identifiable cause found despite thorough investigations. These cases are often referred to as "unexplained stillbirths." Most cases are unexplained. Sometimes stillbirths could be directly linked to the soul's decision not to incarnate in that particular body or lifetime. According to Cayce's readings, a soul may initially agree to incarnate, but at some point before its birth, it may decide that the conditions are not right for fulfilling its spiritual purpose. This could be due to the soul realizing that it is not fully prepared or equipped for the challenges or lessons of that particular life. As a result, the soul does not fully enter the physical body yet, leading to stillbirth. Sometimes an advanced soul will volunteer in entering the physical plane for a few short days or sometimes even a few short months to help someone's karma, not necessarily because it needs to work out its own karma but because in the case of a stillbirth, the parents needs that particular experience for the development of their own individual karma. Experiencing a stillbirth might be part of their own spiritual lessons, such as understanding loss, patience, or other life challenges. Remember that souls have free will in their decisions about incarnation, and sometimes, what may appear as a tragic event in the physical world (like a stillbirth) could be a part of a much larger spiritual plan that at the time, we cannot fully understand from a human perspective. A soul can fulfill its purpose without having to live a long physical life. Remember that time is not the same in the spiritual world as it is here in the physical. A soul can spend hundreds if not thousands of years on the other side, as much time as it wants before making the decision to reincarnate back into the physical world. So in other words, it has a very long time to really think long and hard about reincarnating back into the physical plane. A soul can't predict a change in its environmental conditions or even the decisions of the parents once incarnated.

In the spiritual world, once that individual soul is absolutely sure of reincarnating back into the physical and ready to follow through with its decision, its energy then starts moving in that direction and its karma starts slowly being created and its energy begins to fit into the overall universal pattern. In "Between Life and Death", Dolores

Cannon explains how the universal energy flows using the analogy of going down a water slide. Once the soul's energy starts moving in the direction towards being reincarnated, it's too late to change its mind during that process. It is the equivalent to pouring water down a slide. If you pour water down a slide, you can't collect it again until all of the water runs down the slide and you can only re-collect it in its original state once it reaches the bottom. Once the energy starts moving, it is going down the slide so to speak. Once the soul's energy starts the pattern, it must complete that pattern. Once that pattern is completed you'll return back to the spiritual, in the original state that you left, back at the top of the slide.

Before going down, there's excitement and anticipation, but once that person gets on the slide, they can't stop, and the ride begins, representing the process of being born into a new life. The slide itself symbolizes the physical journey of life. While the individual soul experiences all the thrill and all the challenges of being on the ride (life), it eventually reaches the bottom, which represents death. However, just as someone might jump back in line to ride the slide again, the soul can choose to reincarnate, going through the cycle of life and death repeatedly to learn and grow. If a soul chooses to commit suicide, it disrupts the natural flow. Just like jumping off of a waterslide prematurely, committing suicide can disrupt the natural flow of experiences and lessons the soul was meant to go through in that particular lifetime. By ending one's life early, the soul does not complete the challenges it was set out to face, meaning it may need to return in another lifetime to deal with similar circumstances.

The Three Levels of Mind

There are three levels of **mind** that relate and interconnect with our soul development and its overall journey. There is the **conscious**, the **subconscious**, and the **superconscious**.

The **conscious mind** is that aspect of us that deals with the day-to-day activities, logical and analytical thinking, and the material world.

It's our waking awareness and personality. It is the tool the soul uses to interact with the physical realm by serving as the bridge between the outer world and our inner self. It is through the conscious mind that individuals make choices that shape their life experiences and karmic consequences. It is where we experience our awareness of the material world, our thoughts, decisions, and all of our perceptions of the physical world. The conscious mind is responsible for navigating all of us through this very dense external world, processing all our sensory information, making choices, and interacting with our physical environment. It represents the surface level of awareness and focuses primarily on the physical, rational, and the temporal aspects of life. The reason why the conscious mind helps to navigate through the physical world is because the conscious mind is the **ego**. The ego is the part of the soul that is most directly associated with the conscious, material experience and personal identity. It helps the soul navigate the physical world, giving it a sense of individuality and self-preservation. The ego is a necessary aspect of the soul's existence in the material realm but is not the core of the soul itself. It is primarily focused on survival, personal desires, and maintaining a separate sense of self

The **subconscious mind** is the mind of the soul, a vast reservoir of our memory, emotions, and experiences. The subconscious is not confined by time or space, meaning it stores not only memories from this lifetime but also past-life experiences. It is the realm of our dreams, intuition, and all our emotional responses, and is intimately linked overall with the soul's journey through multiple lifetimes. The subconscious serves as a bridge between the conscious mind and the divine realms. It contains latent knowledge, the hidden desires, and our unresolved issues from past experiences, all of which can influence a person's current life. The subconscious is also where the soul's karmic patterns reside, influencing both behavior and life circumstances. Through practices such as meditation, prayer, and dream interpretation, individuals can access their subconscious mind to heal past wounds, understand their spiritual purpose, and gain deeper insights into their true nature. It can be thought of as being the mind of the soul.

The **superconscious mind** sometimes called the spiritual mind or Christ Consciousness, represents the highest level of awareness and is very closely aligned with that of the divine. It is the realm of universal consciousness, where the individual's mind connects with the collective mind of all creation/God's mind. The superconscious contains the purest form of divine truth and wisdom, untainted by the limitations of the human ego, our personality, or our simple daily material concerns. The superconscious mind is the place where the soul's true purpose and the divine blueprint reside. It is the level of mind in which all individuals can access divine inspiration, higher guidance, and even their innate ability to connect to the Creative Forces or (God). Unlike the subconscious mind, which is shaped by personal experiences and emotions, the superconscious is entirely transcendent, representing the individual's direct link to that of the divine order of the universe.

When individual souls begin to align their conscious mind with their superconscious mind, they begin to experience profound spiritual awakening, guidance, and wisdom. Cayce saw the superconscious as the source of mystical experiences, prophetic insights, and the Christ Consciousness—the state of perfect unity with the divine. It is important to highlight that the superconscious mind is not influenced by earthly things and far from the reach from any earthly influences. In the beginning when those creative forces or when God created us in his image, an aspect of himself which was perfect was shared with us, this was one of those aspects along with the life force or spirit, which serves as the direct link to the creator. True spiritual growth and divine healing occurs when the conscious mind, the subconscious mind, and superconscious mind are harmonized. The conscious mind, guided by the gift of free will, can choose to open itself up to the insights of that of the subconscious and the divine wisdom of the superconscious. Through practices like meditation, prayer, and dream analysis, individuals can then tap into their own subconscious and superconscious minds', thus allowing for a more integrated, holistic understanding of life and their spiritual journey.

It is also important to point out that sometimes the subconscious mind can be indistinguishable from the superconscious mind under certain conditions. The subconscious mind, when in a heightened or spiritually attuned state, can merge with the superconscious mind, which is as stated the mind connected to the divine or Universal Consciousness. The subconscious mind, which stores memories of past lives and deeper wisdom, can access the superconscious mind (or Christ Consciousness) during experiences like deep meditation, trance, dreams, or hypnosis. During these states, the subconscious becomes aligned with the superconscious, thus allowing insights from the divine realms to flow into that person's awareness. This fusion of the subconscious and superconscious mind is central to one's spiritual growth and healing, as it allows individuals to tap into higher wisdom and divine guidance, transcending ordinary waking consciousness. The last thing that I want to clear up pertaining to the soul is the question people ask, "If the soul has always existed, then how can it be created"? Souls were created by God as part of the divine plan, but creation doesn't imply a "beginning" in the linear sense that we typically understand. Souls are aspects of God, and because God is eternal, the souls are also eternal. This means that while souls were created by God, their essence has always existed, since they are derived from the same eternal source as God. The soul is like a "spark" of the divine. Just as a spark from a fire shares the nature of the fire, the soul shares the nature of the divine, which is eternal. In this way, the soul always existed because its essence comes from an eternal source. Gifting a soul with individuality and free will by allowing it to make its own choice to become separate from divine awareness was part of the divine act of creation. In other words, souls were created when God bestowed upon them the ability to choose and act independently of the divine unity. Souls were created in the sense that God gave each of them individual consciousness, free will, and purpose. This "moment" of creation was when the souls became aware of their individuality, but they were still part of the divine, thus retaining their eternal nature.

Chapter 15: Becoming Supernatural; Attuning Ourselves to The Infinite

I want to remind you all that human beings are extremely powerful. Deep inside each and every one of us lays dormant power without direction. You are so much more than just a hardworking employee, a sister, aunt, cousin, brother, uncle, mom or dad. In order for us to tap into the infinite reservoir of power of our supernatural selves it first starts in the mind itself. We all must learn to change and manipulate our own brainwaves to become better versions of our former selves. We will pick back up on consciousness from chapter eight and go just a little deeper into the different stages or levels of consciousness but first let's learn about a few interesting people you may never heard of. There was a woman by the name of Helen Hadsell, **born June 1, 1924 – died October 30, 2010**; she was regarded as the contest queen since she had won seven visits to Paris, won several boats and even a beautiful house along the way. She would just take part in whatever sweepstakes she read about, and she would ultimately win nearly everything she put her mind to. Put it this way; some of us wouldn't stand a chance with her on *"The Price Is Right."* She was known as a psychic in her time and had a Doctorate in *"Metaphysics."* Metaphysics, for those that may not know, are abstract theories of a variety and a multitude of deep spiritual concepts that's not widely accepted by our mainstream scientists and researchers, such as the paranormal, time, space, the human soul, human consciousness etc. Helen Hadsell was able to keep a very positive mindset combined with the extraordinary ability of calling her desires into the material plane to manifest by bending the very fabric of reality. When asked how she was able to win all the time she said it was because of the *"Silva Technique."* The idea that human beings have the ability to manifest desires or intentions into physical reality has been associated with concepts like the law of attraction, positive thinking, and some other spiritual and metaphysical beliefs since ancient times. The proponents of these hidden concepts suggest that the thoughts, beliefs, and emotions of individuals can influence the events and circumstances that we all experience throughout our daily lives.

[Figure] 15.1 Jose Silva

Jose Silva, was an average but very well-known and popular man in his time in the spiritual and psychological world. Silva had worked a long time as a local radio repairman in the early 1940's in his hometown of Laredo, Texas. He was the father of ten children and a former soldier in the United States army. Silva one day began to notice that his children were doing very poorly in school. Using the knowledge he accumulated in his years as a radio repairman and with him working with electricity and deeply understanding the fundamentals of acoustic frequencies, one day Jose Silva had a very groundbreaking thought. Silva understood that by reducing the resistance in a wire, more electrical current will flow through it. So he wondered what he can do to achieve that very same effect in the human brain, removing restrictions allowing consciousness to flow freely. Silva experimented with what we call bio-feedback or also known as neural-feedback, which in psychology and neuroscience circles is the process of hooking up a subject to an EEG machine and monitoring their brain's electrical activity or brain waves. Silva also experimented with hypnosis in combination with the EEG. One day Silva was reading a history book aloud to one of his daughters named Isabelle. He would then put her in a restful, relaxed state or trance and Isabelle would recall back the information seamlessly with a perfect memory, then suddenly, to Silva's amazement, there was something very inexplicable and miraculous that happened. While Silva was thinking of the next question to ask Isabelle, before he could verbally get the question out of his mouth Isabelle would answer that question well before she herself even knew exactly what the question was. Isabelle displayed having telepathic abilities. Soon after this incident Jose Silva wrote to J.B. Rhine out of Duke University, who was very famously known for his research in what we call today E.S.P. (*Extra Sensory Perception*), and said "Doctor, I think I trained my daughter to have E.S.P." Rhine replied and told Silva that couldn't even be possible because she will have to be born with it. Silva disagreed with Rhine and began to teach his other nine children to shift their consciousness into altered states and lo and behold, it worked, proving Rhine wrong. Over time Silva documented his experiments and trained over thirty-nine children in Laredo, Texas as well as some adults. Silva's ingenious technique became well known as ***"The Silva Mind Control Method"*** which became a huge wave across the United States. From a very young age each and every one of us at some point are hyper sensitive to the spiritual or the immaterial world and naturally, as we tend to get older and go through life and all of its experiences of pain and pleasure our innate abilities become suppressed.

Brainwaves

There are five basic types of brainwaves or states of consciousness that we can experience and each state goes in order by frequency. The first state is **Beta** which is approximately between **[16Hz to 30Hz]**. In Beta state, that is what you are experiencing now. You are alert and aware of the things around you in your environment, relaxed and don't feel any sense of harm or danger. You are more so actively engaged in what you are doing, focused and keeping busy. It is a more outward focus. A person who is having a normal conversation will be in low beta while a person debating will be in high beta. It is also the state of experiencing physical sensory input. It is important for us to pay close attention when we are in a high beta trance state because we are not open to learning at all and are regretful afterwards. To put it more simply, if you are in a debate, an argument, or even in the middle of sending a very negative and derogatory text, in that very moment there is absolutely no new information that will reach or be received by the nervous system that isn't proportional or even equal to all the emotions that you are experiencing. Therefore, in that moment if you say or do something that you know you shouldn't do, you feel regretful and start beating yourself up. Esoterically speaking, the beta state is seen as the default waking state that keeps the mind grounded in the material world and outward-focused. It is considered the barrier between ordinary consciousness and higher states of consciousness (such as alpha, theta, and delta waves). In this sense, the beta state is often associated with the illusion of separation from higher spiritual realities and deeper subconscious insights. The beta state is both a tool and a limitation. It represents the conscious mind's ability to focus on the material world, allowing for practical action, mental discipline, and intentional thought projection. However, it can also act as a strong barrier to deeper spiritual experiences and higher consciousness.

HUMAN BRAIN WAVES

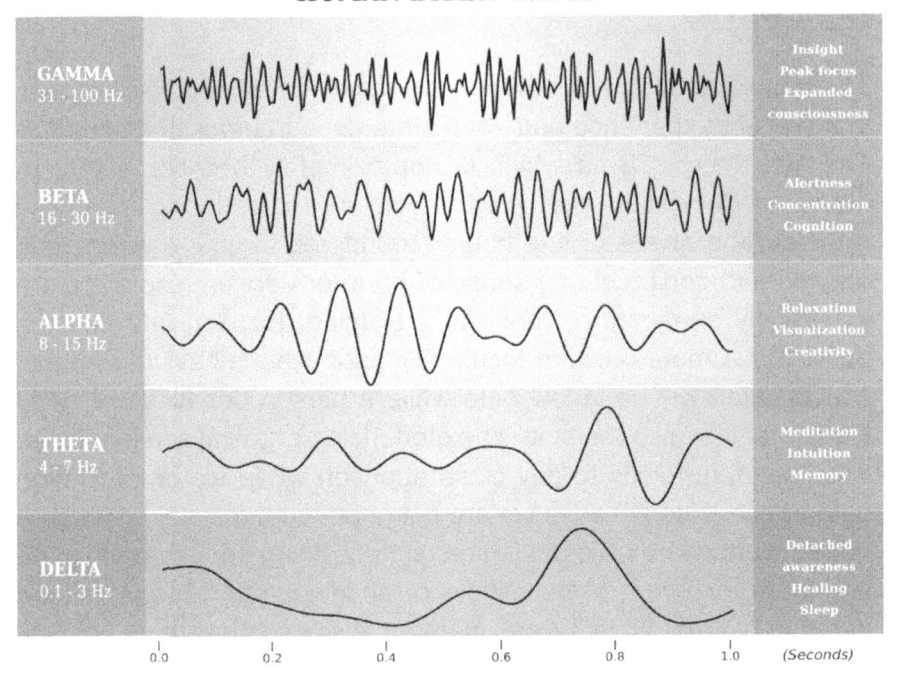

GAMMA 31 - 100 Hz		Insight Peak focus Expanded consciousness
BETA 16 - 30 Hz		Alertness Concentration Cognition
ALPHA 8 - 15 Hz		Relaxation Visualization Creativity
THETA 4 - 7 Hz		Meditation Intuition Memory
DELTA 0.1 - 3 Hz		Detached awareness Healing Sleep

[Figure 15.2]

The second state of our consciousness is called **Alpha**. Alpha state is approximately between [**8Hz to 15Hz**]. This is the beginning of a light meditative state. This is the altered state you will begin to slip into when you are coming out of beta state. This is where you will become physically and mentally relaxed. The mind and the body meet. Alpha state influences our creativity and our intuition. Alpha brain-waves at times tend to be the most prominent around the occipital cortical area of the brain, the visual processing center that lies at the back of the human brain. In other words when we get in a relaxed state while in alpha, one of the positive benefits is that it influences and enhances our own visual abilities, not physically but mentally. Our thoughts and ideas become more vivid to us in turn allowing us to be more creative and imaginative. Once we begin to slowly slip out of a beta consciousness and into an alpha state of consciousness it is here where we start to become an open channel and receptive to the things inside of us rather than outside of us. We began to attune ourselves to something higher.

The next state of consciousness is **Theta**. As we begin to push ourselves and slip deeper into a meditative state and out of alpha consciousness we will then begin to slip into what is known as Theta consciousness. The theta frequency range is approximately between [**4Hz-7Hz**]. This state of consciousness is responsible for influencing our inspirations and our ideas. It can also help us solve difficult and complex problems. This is a deep meditative state and is also the beginning or first stage of sleep. This is one of the most amazing meditative states to experience because in this frequency range we can then begin to tap into and develop a greater sense of our awareness and enhanced perception of the unknown. Thomas Edison for example very easily held over one-thousand patents for inventing some of the most innovative inventions during his time such as the telegraph, light bulb, phonograph, movie camera, and alkaline batteries. Edison would lay down with a metal ball in his hand and a metal plate object on the floor. When he begins to slip into theta consciousness into a light sleep state his hand will drop, the metal ball will drift out of his hand hitting the metal plate object on the floor creating a very loud clang sound that will lead to him waking up, and then he will repeat the process. To put it simply, Edison was purposely dipping himself into a light sleep and waking up continuously over and over. By doing this he was tapping into a theta state of consciousness each time before waking up. What this does is allow the person to tap into greater insight, inspiration, and call forth a much deeper intuitiveness and broader understanding about the things they wouldn't otherwise understand or would have come to in a more normal state of consciousness. Also, there was a famous and world renowned Spanish surrealist artist by the name of Salvador Dali who lived around the same time as Edison, who had a very similar method. Dali, using the very same technique as Edison, but Instead of using a metal ball, Dali would use a simple key to achieve the same result. Famous inventor William Gates II, well known for over a dozen innovative patents would lock himself in his basement, turn off the lights, sit on his desk and close his eyes and would induce himself into a theta state of consciousness. It would seem that some of the most infamous and greatest minds of the early nineteenth century had a very precise understanding of how to manipulate their thought patterns to expand their higher awareness in a way that was kept hidden from the general public.

The next level of our human consciousness is **Delta**. Delta state of consciousness is approximately between **[0.1Hz to 4Hz]**. At this level of consciousness this is where the healing and rejuvenation begins to take its place. This is the state where the body begins to rapidly repair itself on a cellular level. Healing and body repair happens while we sleep which is why sleep is so important. This is the level or state you enter when you are in a very deep meditation or when you are completely asleep. You lose all sense of your physical body and all physical awareness. The delta state is just as mystifying and incredible as theta. You can also program your mind for certain things right before you go to sleep and once you are in a delta state of consciousness your mind will begin to solve problems for you while in delta. Delta is very magical in a sense because the people who operate in or allow themselves to reach a delta state of consciousness will have amazing things happened to them that can't be explained; like walking down the street and finding a one-hundred-dollar bill on the ground, or even playing at a casino and five minutes later win etc. People who operate and function within this frequency range often appear to be extremely lucky and the outcome of their situations always seem to be beneficial for them without them trying, almost like their walking with confidence in God's favor and they know it. It seems that people in this particular state of heightened consciousness are bending the very fabric of reality. Humans can only get the circumstances they claim to seek if there are certain prerequisites that are met first. The manifestation of such circumstances will not occur nor can it be obtained if the prerequisites for getting them are not fully satisfied. Sound familiar? People who walk in this consciousness are walking in what we all call the law of attraction. The mystical effects of coming into this consciousness occurs because everything in creation is bound by unseen laws and humans can tap into the forces that govern these laws by knowing the requirements and conditions that need to be met. As I have stated earlier, the conditions will not materialize if the prerequisites for getting them are not satisfied.

I know what you may be thinking. You are wondering how a person can be awake and still do all these crazy things if a delta state of consciousness is associated with being fully asleep. Although delta waves are usually most associated with being or falling asleep, this frequency range can also be generated in a waking state as well by some experienced practitioners of meditation. The very concept of meditation doesn't mean that you have to close your eyes and cross your legs. There are different forms of meditation and one of those forms is called "**Walking Meditation**" which is simply the practice of meditating throughout the day while you are awake and engaged in activity. This practice is no different from a basketball player in a critical moment slipping into an alpha state of consciousness before hitting a game winning shot. To be clear, we all have a combination of brain-waves which can all be active at the very same time either while you are awake or while you are asleep. However, the most dominant frequency or Brain-wave that is the strongest and the most active at the time determines the state of consciousness of that person

The highest level of our human consciousness that we know of is called **Gamma.** Gamma frequency range is approximately between [**30Hz to 100Hz**]. During a Gamma state of consciousness, you are tapped into such a heightened state that everything in your inner world is just as real as everything in your outer world. In fact, you wouldn't even be able to tell the difference. Once a gamma state of consciousness is achieved the kundalini energy that sits at the base of the spinal cord begins to rise up through the spine in a serpent like motion until it reaches a gate at the bottom of the brainstem which is called the **Thalamic Gate**. When this gate opens, there is an energetic rush of kundalini energy that begins to flood the pineal gland. When the pineal gland becomes activated, because of the compressed pressure of energy and the rush of neurons that is flowing directly through it, the pineal gland then begins to produce an electromagnetic field. This electromagnetic energy that is in the pineal gland begins to activate and it heightens the entire central nervous system. It's similar to taking your headlights which are already turned on and switching it to a high beam. Kundalini energy is simply the energy that gets trapped and stuck within our own bodies. This energy originally comes from the brain. When we stress, when we feel fear, anger, jealousy, etc., our brains not only produce the necessary corresponding hormones and corresponding chemicals that are equal to those low vibratory thoughts and emotions, but *also* produce the corresponding *energies* necessary that are equal to those thoughts and emotions. These energies are what get trapped in our four lower energy centers. To put it simply, all a kundalini awakening is, is the ancient practice of releasing those trapped or stuck energies and sending them back to the brain from whence they came. Back up to heaven. Let us take a long at the following Bible scripture:

Matthew 18:1-5

At the same time came the disciples unto Jesus, saying, who is the greatest in the kingdom of heaven?

And Jesus called a little child unto him, and set him in the midst of them,

And said, Verily I say unto you, except ye be converted, and become as little children, ye shall not enter into the kingdom of heaven.

Whosoever therefore shall humble himself as this little child, the same is greatest in the kingdom of heaven.

Some may read this book and realize all the information they have been missing in their life that points directly back to Source and say to themselves that they might not feel or be smart enough to get closer to God/Source. You don't have to be a very highly intelligent person to start wanting to become closer to God or Source or simply wanting to have a relationship with the divine. Look at it this way: See, the left brain is considered the **male consciousness**. The left brain deals with logic, analytical thought, linear thought, reason, scientific and mathematical thinking while the right side of the human brain is considered the **female consciousness.** The left side of our brains' deals with several different functions as well such being; creativity, randomness, emotions, pattern recognition, holistic thinking which is seeing things in its entirety, being able to see interconnected relationships and the overall bigger picture as well as having the ability to display compassion. See, you don't have to remember spiritual scripture or learn how to quote the Bible from front to back. Intellect **IS NOT** intelligence. Intellect only deals with one side of the brain which is the male side. Therefore, to put it simply, intellect is only one side of understanding. In order for one to ultimately obtain or display true intelligence both the male and female consciousness must interconnect. The bipolar energies of both sides of the brain must be in complete coherence. In other words, true intelligence is obtained when logic and reason comes into a marriage with compassion, intuitiveness and creativity. This synthesis creates an awareness that transcends the limitations of the material world and thus taps into higher wisdom. This balance reflects a deeper spiritual principle of duality and harmony, where wholeness is achieved through the complete merging of opposites.

The Power Of Thought And Programing

We have to take better care of our mental state of being. How we think, what we think and the things we react to have enough power to influence physical reality. For example; once we begin to stress, stress hormones down regulate genes and create disease, this is a known scientific and spiritual truth that has been proven time and time again. Oftentimes we get so used to doing things in repetition everyday that when we finally wake up, at some point our body remembers and knows how to do things much better than our brain. In other words, if I wake up every day and grab a cup of coffee; that means that at some point in my life I've stopped thinking about it upon awakening and my body automatically got out of bed and started making coffee. This is what we have to be aware of. We should never want the body to become the brain. Your body should never take over the function or title of being the *thinker*. Oftentimes we never notice it because it happens on a subconscious level, but by living by a repetitive routine, we literally trade our *free will* for a *program*. Majority of people wake up every day and begin thinking about things that happened the day before. Ninety percent of our thoughts are from our past experiences and as Dr. Joe Dispenza teaches; the brain itself is just a record of the past. If we wake up everyday thinking of the same things; not only are you starting your day thinking in the past, but those very same memories are tied to people, problems, places and things and each of those memories are tied to an emotion or even several emotions. To put it simply, if emotions are the end product of our past experiences; and I feel those same emotions from those past thoughts and past problems I had the day before, that means that the moment I start to feel those past emotions the very next day I wake up; my entire state of being is operating and functioning in the past. Every single fiber of my entire physical being is now vibrating from a past experience. I am in yesterday all over again. As Dr. Dispenza brilliantly points out, a familiar past will sooner or later become a predictable future. We all have to teach our bodies not to live in the predictable, which are known outcomes, but live in the unpredictable which are unknown outcomes. Your environment shouldn't create your thinking but your thinking should create your environment. So to sum it all up, when we live by our past experiences; the same thoughts prompt the same decisions, the same decisions result in the same actions, and those same actions will then result in those very same past old experiences, which in turn cause the same **EMOTIONS**.

Afterword

Dear Reader,

As you close the final pages of "Laws of the Universe," I want to extend my heartfelt gratitude to you for embarking on this journey with me, exploring the interconnectedness of spirituality and science in a way that has never been done before. Your willingness to delve into the depths of these concepts and to consider the harmonious relationship between the two is a considerable testament to your open-mindedness and thirst for understanding. I truly commend you for your dedication to the pursuit of knowledge and wisdom.

Throughout the many pages of this book, we have explored the profound connection between the spiritual and scientific realms, delving into topics that have long been considered separate or even contradictory. We have seen how the fundamental laws of the universe, both in the realms of physics and metaphysics, are harmonious and unified. The realization that the microcosm and the macrocosm, the seen and the unseen, are inextricably linked can be a powerful catalyst for personal growth and transformation.

In our very deep exploration, we have uncovered the truth that the universe operates in accordance with certain laws and forces that govern not only the physical world but also the metaphysical and spiritual dimensions. From the law of attraction to the law of karma, we have seen first-hand how these cosmic principles play a very significant role in our everyday lives. Embracing and understanding that these unseen and divine laws can help you navigate your journey with greater insight and purpose. But the journey does not end here. As you close this book, I want to remind you that the vigorous pursuit of spiritual awareness and understanding is an ongoing, lifelong endeavor. Just as the infinite universe continually expands and evolves, so too should our spiritual growth. Your soul is a very precious gem, a beacon of light in the vast cosmos, and it deserves your attention and nurturing. Continuing to develop your very soul, your essence, expanding your overall consciousness, and deepening your connection with the universe/*Source* is not only a very personal endeavor but also a collective one. By doing so, you contribute to the greater good, fostering a deeper sense of unity and compassion in our world. Remember that you are a very vital and significant part of the tapestry of all existence, and your growth and understanding ripple out to touch the lives of those around you.

In your long quest for spiritual enlightenment, you may encounter challenges, doubts, and moments of uncertainty. This is natural, for the path of the soul is not always smooth or well-lit. However, trust in the wisdom of the universe and the power of your own inner light. Just as the stars shine in the darkest of nights, your soul's brilliance can guide you through the challenges you encounter.

So, dear reader, as you carry the insight and wisdom gained from "Laws of the Universe" with you, remember that you are a co-creator of your own reality. You have the power to shape not just your own life, but the world around you through your own thoughts and by your own actions and intentions. Your journey is a very sacred one, and I encourage you to continue exploring, seeking, and growing. May God's wisdom and your very own inner knowing, guide you on this remarkable adventure. Your path is unique, and the destination is ever-evolving. Embrace the journey with an open heart, a very curious mind, and a solid steadfast commitment to the development of your soul. At every step in your journey, allow yourself to be a channel for *Source* to work through.

With immense gratitude and warmest wishes,

Kevin S. Black

Acknowledgments

This book, "Laws of the Universe," would not have been possible without the guiding hand of a force beyond my understanding. I am deeply grateful for the divine inspiration that filled me with ambition and purpose, leading me to embark on this unexpected journey of writing. It was a calling I never anticipated, but one that I embraced with an open heart.

I must acknowledge that the inception of this book came in a moment of divine intervention. I vividly remember that day when a surge of energy, like an electric charge filled with ambition and inspiration, coursed through me. It was a call from the depths of my subconscious, whispering that this book was meant to come into physical manifestation for a higher purpose. I cannot explain where these feelings originated, but I trusted the wisdom of my subconscious, which often knows what the conscious mind cannot fathom.

I embarked on this endeavor with a sense of purpose and a profound understanding that I was meant to share the spiritual concepts and knowledge that I had acquired over time. The topics I delved into were ones I had explored extensively, and I felt compelled to bridge the gap between the esoteric and the everyday.

I am immensely grateful for the support and encouragement I received along the way. My supervisor at the time, Lieutenant Foster, played a pivotal role in nurturing the seeds of inspiration within me. Our deep contemplations of the unseen world and discussions of esoteric concepts were instrumental in shaping the content of this book. Her constant encouragement and belief in the importance of this work were a driving force behind its completion. She even affectionately nicknamed me "Siri" for my seemingly endless knowledge of spiritual matters.

To all of those who have been a part of this long journey, whether through inspiration, encouragement, or even support, I extend my heartfelt thanks. Your presence in my life has been a blessing, and your belief in this endeavor has been a fuel source of motivation and strength. This book is a very testament to the unseen power of inspiration, intuition, and the extraordinary connections that exist between us all.

I would like to express my heartfelt gratitude to my dear friend and brother, Jeston Vincent, for his unwavering support and the profound impact he has had on my spiritual journey. Jeston, your friendship has been a source of inspiration, enlightenment, and growth throughout the writing of this book.

Our deep spiritual conversations have been nothing short of transformative. They have challenged me to expand my horizons, to venture beyond the boundaries of my own beliefs, and to see the spiritual world through fresh eyes. You possess a unique gift for igniting the flames of curiosity and exploration within me, pushing me to think beyond the ordinary and the expected.

The way you challenge my spiritual mind keeps me on my toes and encourages me to continuously seek a deeper understanding of the spiritual realms. It's a remarkable example of "iron sharpening iron," as our discussions inspire and elevate my thinking, and I am eternally grateful for the wisdom and insights you share.

In those moments when I have found myself lost and entangled in the labyrinth of my own thoughts, you have consistently provided a different perspective and a new way of perceiving the spiritual world. Your guidance and support have been invaluable on this journey, and I consider myself fortunate to have you as a friend and spiritual companion.

Thank you, Jeston, for your unwavering friendship, your spiritual wisdom, and your boundless enthusiasm for exploring the mysteries of the universe. Your presence in my life has been a gift, and I am honored to acknowledge your significant role in the creation of this book.

I also want to take the time out to express my deepest gratitude to Kevin J. Todeschi. Thank you for generously taking the time to humbly share your invaluable perspective on the material in this book. Your influence and dedication to spiritual exploration and esoteric wisdom have inspired thousands within the spiritual and esoteric community. It is through your extensive work and teachings all over the world for the past 40 years that a profound channel has been created, thus allowing individuals like myself to significantly grow and develop their spiritual awareness. Thank you so much for your patience and relentless commitment to the endless pursuit of knowledge and enlightenment.

With deep appreciation and gratitude,

Kevin S. Black

Made in the USA
Las Vegas, NV
25 June 2025